THE REFINERY

FAITH REFINED THROUGH TESTS AND TRIALS

Written By:

RITA WILSON

TABLE OF CONTENTS

ACKNOWLEDGMENTS

I dedicate this book to my mom and dad. Ma, thank you for always being there through the thick and the thin. When no one was around or even understood, you were there. You taught me how to go to Christ first. You showed me that no one is perfect except Jesus. When I didn't trust or understand your advice, God showed me that you were right. Oftentimes, we have been through our own refinement of relationships. But God! I understand now, more than ever, why God gave me you as a mother. You are my best friend! I am honored to be your daughter. I love you with all my heart.

Dad, at first, I thought we had a completely imperfect father-daughter relationship. I was forced to seek other men to fulfill the void I thought I was looking for in you. All the while, as I grew to know and understand you, I realized how much of an amazing person you really are. I remember a few years back when we were on the verge of losing you. During that time, I recognized how much I valued having you in my life. I am blessed to see our relationship grow. You are the perfect dad for me! The Lord has shown me how much we have in common. From jogging and biking to running our first marathon together and now writing, there is no denying we are so much alike! I am honored to walk in your footsteps as an author. Dad, I love you!

To my siblings, cousins, aunties, uncles, friends, and church family, thank you so much for being there for me.

Ultimately, to Christ, my Lord—when I had no one, you were everything. All my life, hopes, and dreams are in your hands. You have given me beauty for ashes. With this book, I give glory and honor to You, my Lord and Savior. Thank You, Jesus!

MESSAGE FROM DAD

L ife for a Christian is a gift from the Divine. Step outside the comfort of your home and look at the wonderful creation that surrounds you. The wind that brushes your face. The air you breathe, none of which were man made. The ground from under your feet and the multitudes of creatures living underneath have been there since the time of creation. Ever thought of that?

The flock of birds who flew by while you are standing on the green grass are doing so in an impeccable order or perfect formation. Could some cataclysmic disorder produce such orderly and disciplined creatures?

Lift up your head and look at the horizon. More wonders, the sun in the morning, and the moon and the stars at night. If you live close to the ocean, take a curious look at the rolling waves coming from afar to abruptly wash up on the shoreline. Could a cataclysmic event produce such soothing, rhythmic and orderly sounds?

The beaten path of parents is often followed by their children. These gifts from God learn obedience to the scriptures. By doing so, our children honor their mother and father. Raised in the Church, we show them the ways of the Lord. What they hear and read while practicing God's commandments, are the solid foundation upon which they could always rely on. Living the Christian life is like long distance running. It is not made for sprinters who wear themselves out after the first mile and quit.

I am obviously very proud of my daughter's many achievements. However, by writing this book she had reached a summit that could not be denied. I hope you enjoy it.

-   Love, Dad

FOREWORD

I had the pleasure of meeting Rita at my Writers Retreat in the summer of 2022. When she arrived, I sensed she was wrestling with the thought of putting her book out there. She seemed to have some reservations and hesitancies regarding sharing the message God placed on her heart. Yet, despite these fears, Rita took a bold leap of faith. She traveled all the way to Sarasota, Florida, invested in herself, and stepped into obedience by committing to the process of writing her story.

Through the journey of writing this book, I've watched Rita undergo a profound transformation. I have seen her embrace the refining process—an experience that has shaped the message she now shares with conviction, rooted in truth and purity. This book is not just the fruit of hard work; it results from her willingness to be shaped by God's will, and that speaks volumes about her faith and courage.

Like Rita, we all go through seasons of sanctification, often uncomfortable, but ultimately designed to shape us into the reflection of holiness that God calls us to. The Bible reminds us in 1 Peter 1:16, "Be holy, because I am holy," and it is a lifelong journey that requires the help of the Holy Spirit.

Rita, thank you for being an example of obedience and perseverance. This book is a testament to God's faithfulness, and I pray it encourages every reader to embrace their own journey of refinement with courage and faith.

Sincerely,

Karolyne Roberts
Author & CEO of The Writers Retreat
www.WritersRetreat.com

PREFACE

In 2018, I was inspired to write a book about my life. God immediately gave me a name and title to start. *The Refinery*. I thought to myself, *"Haven't I heard about this before? It sounds like there is a book or something I have seen out there that has this name."* Still, the Holy Spirit was telling me to write. There were times I would forget about or neglect writing this book—due to the circumstances or distractions in life. Then, a situation, conversation, or scripture reference would bring it to remembrance and spark the fire in me to write again. So, here it is—*The Refinery*.

Upon researching the definition of refinery, there were various words to describe it, such as, a place for refining or processing materials. However, an overarching commonality defined refinery as, *a place where substances in their natural state are made pure* (Cambridge Dictionary, 2025).

The refining process involves removing something, such as dirt, metal and other impurities or unwanted material; to improve or perfect by pruning or polishing (Merriam-

Webster Dictionary, 2025). I am here to tell you that God is my refinery. Through the Holy Spirit, He has purified me and removed (and still is removing) impurities from me in order for me to be used for His glory. I pray that you open your heart to receive what I am about to share. I will be taking you through a journey of personal refinement, through God, in my life. May He receive all the glory and honor through this book. In Jesus' precious and holy name. Amen.

INTRODUCTION

s previously mentioned, a refinery is described as a place where substances in their natural state are made pure. You can refine something by removing impurities or unwanted elements from it. Bible Gateway's Encyclopedia of the Bible includes the terms 'refiner' and 'refining,' typically in reference to metals. Refined gold or silver has historically been known as more precious and expensive. *"Why does gold need to be refined?"* you might be asking.

Gold does not exist in its purest form, naturally. Metal is extracted from its ores, which are mined on earth. Gold obtained after the mining process isn't pure. This gold is often mixed with many impurities that need to be removed. *"Well then, how are they removed?"* you may be thinking. There are various techniques to refine gold. Many of these techniques include processes to extract, isolate, and purify the gold until its final refinement state. One of the oldest and most common methods involves immersing gold in fire; then, impurities rise to the top and one skims them off (dross). The temperatures needed to refine gold are so hot that it can become uncomfortable or even dangerous for those handling the metal. However, after the fire dies down, and the dross skims off, the gold comes out shining brighter than ever.

Although there are several methods involved in the refinement process, an overarching purpose is to separate the desired compound from the undesired compound(s) for it to be completely pure. For the purposes of this book and applying the terminology of refinery to my own life, the refinement process will be broken down into four sections: 1) EXTRACTION, 2) ISOLATION, 3) PURIFICATION, and 4) REFINEMENT.

1) EXTRACTION is defined as the action of taking or pulling out something, especially using effort or force (Oxford Dictionary, 2023).

2) ISOLATION is defined as the process of separation of one substance from another substance to obtain a pure or uncontaminated state (Oxford, 2024; Merriam-Webster, 2025).

3) PURIFICATION is defined as the process of removing contaminants or unwanted impurities from something (Oxford, 2024; Dictionary.com, 2025).

4) REFINEMENT is defined as the process of improving something by making small changes to bring it to a fine or pure state (Oxford, 2024; Dictionary.com, 2025).

All these processes are intertwined and represent the primary goal—*REFINERY*.

CHAPTER 1: BIBLICAL EXAMPLES OF REFINEMENT

In ancient biblical days, the gold-refining process involved crushing the mine ore, pounding it into powder, and then taking it through frequent washings and cleansings. These washings remove a large amount of unwanted, non-metallic elements, leaving only the metallic elements behind. Various Bible references figuratively use the refining of certain precious metals to demonstrate a kind of test or trial God's children face.

If they are of the right metal, the dross will finally be blown away, leaving pure, shining metal. In the book of 1 Peter chapter 1, Peter writes, "...*In this you rejoice, though now for a little while, if necessary, you have been grieved by various trials, so that the tested genuineness of your faith—more precious than gold that perishes though it is tested by fire—may be found to result in praise and glory and honor at the revelation of Jesus Christ...*" (1 Peter 1:6-7 ESV). Peter is talking about what many of us can relate to in this Christian walk—tests and trials. However, he shares that these tests are for a bigger purpose— REFINEMENT.

Before going through my refinement journey, I find it important to first look at some examples of character refinement in the Bible. This will help us see how God allows refinement to purify and sanctify our character, drawing us closer in intimacy with Him. Every person has, is, or will go through some type of refinement in their lifetime. The scriptures are filled with people having their character refined by God, allowing challenging obstacles to transform them and showing the miraculous hand of God in their refinement process.

Job

First, let's look at a biblical character named Job. In the book of Job, the prologue starts off defining Job as 'blameless' and a man of complete integrity. He feared God and stayed away from evil (Job 1:1). You may think, *"Well, it seems Job was already refined."* And you may be right, outwardly looking. In the modern-day world, he would be the 'perfect Christian.' Likely in the position of rank as a bishop or something similar. He was also extremely wealthy. Looking from the outer perspective, many who knew Job knew he was indeed a blessed man. They would see him as 'arriving' and desired to be and have things similar to Job.

Job was sacrificial and obedient towards God. So, why did he have to go through a refining? Did he at all even need it? Looking from the outside in, it would be easy to say, *"No, he did not need it…"* However, God's plans and thoughts are always higher than our own (Isaiah 55:8).

Looking at the *why*, we start with Satan. Do you know he is an accuser of the brethren (Revelation 12:10)? He walks around day and night trying to accuse one of us, God's holy people. Why? Because he hates us. He hates us because we are

God's. We are the apple of God's eyes (Psalms 17:8). Ultimately, he hates us because he hates God. With Job, this was no different. Satan, the hater of all haters, came before God with accusations. Ironically, it wasn't Satan that mentioned Job; it was God. I believe God was using this opportunity to test Job. He knew what the outcome would be. Refinement does not always mean you have done wrong; it may mean that God wants to take you to the next level. With this, He must put you through the test. It is not a test for you to suffer, but for you to succeed by depending on Him.

With that 'name drop' of God mentioning Job, came Satan accusing Job and ultimately blaming God for it! God had placed a hedge of protection over Job, where Satan couldn't enter. He knew these boundaries and had to abide by them. However, he still wanted to test God and accuse him in his stealthy way by saying the reason he fears God is because God gives him everything. He spoils him. You see, it seems our normal tests come, and then things pan out, but for Job, it was the opposite. Things were going great, and then the tests came. Initially, God gave Satan the authority to do whatever he wanted except harm him physically.

Most of the book is about Job's deep suffering. We can only imagine the actual suffering Job experienced. Yet one thing is for sure, God was with him through this process, watching over him. During this refinement, Job never sinned by blaming God (Job 1:22). Was he in deep suffering? Yes! Did he have all the rights to get upset, likely so—but he knew the God he served. He had an intimate relationship with God.

At some point, Satan returns to God, and God allows Satan to strike him with boils. Not only has he lost everything, but his wife also encourages him to curse God and die. He is alone! God has isolated him. During this time, Job never blamed God. In his anguish, he questions his existence. Job chapter 3 verses 13, 16 [NLT version] reads,

"...Had I died at birth, I would now be at peace ...
Why wasn't I buried like a stillborn child, like a baby
who never lives to see the light?"

He could hardly eat or talk. During this suffering, his friends came and questioned his innocence.

Job has gone down in history as the ultimate refinement. What was he refined from; you may ask? The test of righteousness, maybe? A way to prove that he was of God's, no matter what? Ultimately, I believe God was refining Job's mindset in expectations of only receiving blessings from God and not the trials. How many of us can relate to this? We come to faith, trusting that it will be rainbows and butterflies. We believe everything will be perfect. However, God never said it would be easy. In fact, Jesus says, *"Take up your cross and follow me"* (Matthew 16:24). Either way, Job went through the grueling refining process. I believe Job had passed the test of being refined from thinking he knew more than God. Towards the end of the book, Job repents of his fallacy in being a human, falling short of perfection in his own efforts. Job 42 reads, *"Surely, I spoke of things I did not understand, things too wonderful for me to know"* (Job 42:3). Job humbled himself before God in his imperfections. Because of this, God blessed him abundantly; restoring his fortune to twice as much as before (Job 42:10)! So, you see, in the refinery of Job, he was more blessed in the second part of his life than before.

King David

A nother biblical example of the refining process is that of King David. King David was a man after God's own heart (1 Samuel 13:14), yet he had terrible sins. Prior to him becoming king, David was a shepherd boy. He was the son of Jesse from the tribe of Judah. King David's refinement started well before he was crowned king. God was preparing him in the fields by being a shepherd over the sheep.

From the anointing of king by the prophet Samuel, to the actual days of reign as king, David encountered many points of refinement. David had to go through a process of persecution, loneliness, and tests of his loyalty to God, prior to being appointed king. His refinement period began when he came across the Philistine Goliath from Gath. To note, David was not only a shepherd boy, but he was also the youngest of all his other brothers, who were enlisted in the Israelite Army, led by King Saul. David, not a part of the army, was following his father Jesse's instructions to bring them food and check on them to see how they were doing. However, this one-time David came, he heard the mockery and boldness of a giant from Gath—Goliath. Many of the Israelites were afraid and fled with fear when they saw him. But David was not. He asked one of the army men standing by, *"Who is this uncircumcised Philistine, that he should defy the armies of the living God?"* (I Samuel 17:26).

David's heart was for the Lord. He had confidence in the mighty power of the King of kings. He was in disbelief that there would be anyone bold enough to stand against the all-powerful, almighty One.

When Israel's King Saul received word that David wanted to fight Goliath, Saul looked at his appearance and noted that David was a mere boy. But David's heart burned with the fire and boldness for the Lord. You see, even before this appointed time, God was preparing David to fight in battle. Thinking of him as a shepherd boy, you would think that all he knew was how to tend sheep. However, David showed that tending sheep came with a lot of other skills.

1 Samuel 17:34-35 (NIV) reads, *"...But David said to Saul, your servant has been keeping his father's sheep. When a lion or a bear came and carried off a sheep from the flock, I went after it, struck it and rescued the sheep from its mouth. When it turned on me, I seized it by its hair, struck it and killed it. Your servant has killed both the lion and bear; this uncircumcised Philistine will be like one of them...The Lord who rescued me from the paw of the lion*

and the paw of the bear will rescue me from the hand of this

Philistine..."

David had seen God do some miraculous things during his lifetime. This gave him the confidence and boldness that he had during this very moment. His next moment was coming up against Goliath with a rock and a slingshot. One of the most powerful parts of this was David saying to the Philistine, *"...You come against me with sword and spear and javelin, but I come against you in the name of the Lord Almighty..."* (1 Samuel 17:45). God used David to triumph over the enemy that day. This was a monumental highlight of David in scripture, prior to him becoming King of Israel. *"How is this refinement?"* you may ask. It is part of the testing. God was refining David while tending to the sheep. He used his everyday experiences to prepare for a pivotal time in Israel's history—David becoming king. David was walking in his anointing and developing into the king we all knew him to become.

This also allowed many people to know who David was prior to him being king. Something God was orchestrating, all for His perfect will to be done. As the story goes, David was appointed to a high rank in the army, led by King Saul. At this time, King Saul realized God was with David and had left him. This began a time of King Saul's jealousy and envy towards David.

Do you realize that during the refining process, people who were once with you and for you may no longer be there? They will be envious and jealous of you. Having God's anointing will bring you to places before kings; however, the journey is never easy—in this case, especially for David. Many of the moments prior to David becoming king involved him running from King Saul. Even Jonathan, King Saul's son, a true brother and friend to David, helped David escape his father's revenge. King Saul recognized God's anointing on David's life. It was evident. There was nothing he nor anyone else could do to stop it.

The next phase of David's life was running from his enemies. This was his point of isolation. I believe it prepared David for moments of his life when he became king and encountered many enemies, even in his own household. One thing to note about the times that King Saul went after David is the deep, genuine reverence he had for Saul. Although Saul was attempting to kill him, David honored the fact that this was a man appointed by God to be king. Even when King Saul was searching from place to place and barely missing him at times, hiding in caves.

During this time of instability and isolation in David's life, he had some of the most intimate times with the Lord. Many of his actions were directly related to hearing from and/or having reverence for the Lord (1 Samuel 23). Something to note is that, during this time, David was escaping to hills and strongholds. Although in the physical sense of the locations, it may have also been in the spiritual sense. David was away from anything comfortable. He was in the hands of the Living God. A stronghold is a fortified place that protects against attack. God was David's stronghold. His guidance and instructions were all David had at this time in life. He could only place his trust in the Lord. During this time, God continuously refined him into a man after His own heart.

David maintained loyalty to King Saul, even after Saul died and he succeeded him as King of Israel. As the new king, David inherited all of Saul's enemies along with his own. His continuous battles against the Philistines, Syrians and internal opposition from his own people, were pruning experiences that God used to refine his character, and make him successful in all he did. He was victorious in his defeats, so the Lord made David famous and gave him victory everywhere he went (2 Samuel 8:13-14). David even honored King Saul by showing kindness to the grandson of Saul and son of Jonathan, Mephibosheth (2 Samuel 9).

Despite God's blessings and King David's refinement, his character still needed pruning. The temptations of lust came lurking through. When he was supposed to be going off to war, he found himself lusting after another man's wife, Bathsheba. This is, unfortunately, the most shameful moment of King David's life. It was his pitfall.

We know that he not only committed adultery with another man's wife, but he also murdered the man, having found out she was pregnant. All of this displeased the Lord. This was one of the first moments in the Bible that we see King David displease the Lord. Ironically, when everything around him was going well.

During tough times and isolation, he drew close to the Lord. Yet, as things turned around and were going well, it seemed like distractions and sin crept in—drawing him into his own desires and solutions, instead of the Lord's. If we look back at human life, in the beginning, it was human nature for us to mess things up when we go outside the will of God. To follow our fleshly desires instead of His. And it happens when we least expect it.

Because of the sins that King David committed, the Lord had promised calamity, and that the sword would never depart his household (2 Samuel 12:10-11). This, indeed, was the case. But David knew the Lord; he had a direct and intimate relationship with Him. Upon receiving God's message of punishment through Nathan, David, being God's son, knew he could directly approach Him. He fell in repentance before the Lord.

Although his firstborn son from Bathsheba died, when David heard the news of his child's death—he went into the house of the Lord and worshiped (2 Samuel 12:20). Not something that makes sense, right? Well, King David knew the Lord had made his final decision. He knew the Lord had all power in His hand to let the child live or die—and in the end, the Lord chose for the child to die.

Thankfully many other children came about, from King David's lineage. This is where we see King David's most pure and refined state. He dedicated himself to the Lord. After this point, we can see the humbleness in all he did. He had a heart for the Lord and for his children. However, he understood that all things that Nathan mentioned from the Lord would come to pass. King David placed all of it in God's hands.

He knew the Lord, now more than ever, had all power and authority. Many may say that the later days of King David were intense, gruesome, and maybe even sorrowful. However, I believe that because of the refinement through tests and trials, the Lord gave King David more wisdom and grace than ever before. He also gave King David another son to carry his name and be known as the wisest man that ever lived.

Esther and Ruth

Unlike biblical characters such as King David, we do not know much about the lives of Esther and Ruth, other than the few chapters within each book of the Bible. However, I saw the need to place some biblical women as examples of refinement, for relatability and applicability of how God can refine us, as women.

Esther

The little we know about Queen Esther, prior to her coming on the scene, is that she was a Jew from the tribe of Benjamin. She lived with her cousin Mordecai from the city of Susa. Her Hebrew name was Hadassah, which Mordecai later commanded her to switch prior to entering the King's palace, so that no one would identify her as a Jew. We know very little about Esther's childhood, except that her mother and father (Abihail, the uncle of Mordecai) died, and she was taken as Mordecai's own daughter (Esther 2:7). In this, we can assume that Esther had gone through various trials early in life. One can only imagine not having your mother and father in your life growing up. Looking further into scripture, Mordecai was carried into exile from Jerusalem by Nebuchadnezzar among those taken captive with Jehoiachin, king of Judah.

In this, we can imagine that Esther and her parents may have been in the same situation. Hence, Mordecai takes her in after their death. Esther had a lovely figure and was beautiful (Esther 2:7). We can learn from scripture that names have meaning. In looking at the Hebrew origin name, Hadassah means *myrtle tree*, which is symbolically associated with peace, love, and prosperity.

As a result of the king's order to the city of Susa, Esther was taken into the king's palace. She won favor with Hegai, who had charge of the harem, and was pleased with her (Esther 2:9). Esther's wisdom likely developed through the years under Mordecai's care and guidance. Not only was she beautiful and favored by God, but she was obedient to the instructions of Mordecai not to tell anyone that she was a Jew. This was likely very difficult for young Esther. She knew her life's circumstances and what she had endured—being completely cut off from her family, everything familiar, and her very name. However, Esther was stronger than how she appeared. She knew her identity came from the Lord. She even won the favor of the King and became Queen Esther.

God had blessed Queen Esther abundantly through the trials and sufferings that were against her. He honored her humility and obedience. However, God's plans were higher and wiser than what she could imagine. Like Joseph in scripture, who rose to a high position in Egypt after his captivity to save his family, Queen Esther's high rank and position prepared her for this moment. She was to save her people from the hatred of Haman's plot to kill all Jews. Haman was a highly ranked nobleman. Next to King Xerxes, he was the second in power and authority, to the point where he wore the king's signet ring. This allowed for Haman's plot to destroy the Jews to go into effect. However, Mordecai, the cousin of Queen Esther, persuaded Esther to help.

Something important to note, Esther not only had the wisdom from her cousin Mordecai raising her, but she also had the wisdom of God. She knew her assignment was to help save her people. How she went about it was likely the wisest thing of all. Esther was not emotional. She was not moved by fear or anger. She knew how to present herself to the Lord first. She knew the power of fasting and prayer. Ultimately, Esther won the approval of King Xerxes, which led to the execution of Haman, the one attempting to kill the Jews.

Through it all, we can see the refining process of Queen Esther being boldness, meekness, and wisdom. This goes to show, the refinement process doesn't mean trials won't come.

In fact, they may get worse. How you handle the trials is what matters. Esther was a beautiful example of this.

Ruth

Another biblical example of refinement is through the story of Ruth. Like Esther, we know little about Ruth's early life as a child. However, we can see that Ruth dealt with tragedy similarly to Esther. Ruth sadly experienced the death of her father, brother-in-law, and husband. She, her sister, and mother-in-law, Naomi, now had to figure out the next steps in life. During the times of Ruth, men provided for the household, and women were the keepers of the home.

Losing the three men in their family, who would be the providers, placed them in a situation of poverty and hopelessness. Naomi even tells her daughters-in-law to leave to go back to their own homes and family, as they were Moabite women. However, Ruth refuses. She had a heart for the God of her husband that she had grown to know. Not much is known about her family, but Ruth was determined to stay with her mother-in-law instead of returning home. She found her identity in the God of her husband. Naomi takes a journey back to the home of Bethlehem. Ruth now saw her identity in the one true God. She became a worker in the fields of Boaz, gleaning until evening (Ruth 2:17). She was bold. Similar to Esther, she left behind what she knew, to become a foreigner somewhere she did not know. She immediately won favor in the eyes of Boaz, who had his workers leave some stalks for her to pick up (Ruth 2:16).

Ruth was a hard worker and didn't expect anything from anyone around her. She did not play the victim or think that anyone owed her anything. She worked in the fields diligently with the other harvest workers, gathering grain until the end of the barley harvest. This wasn't just any harvest; it was the first harvest of the year. A time for people to bring in their first fruits to the Lord. Thinking of this symbolic meaning, God had something to show us here about Ruth. She was diligent not only towards her mother-in-law but also towards God. She was bringing in her best as a servant of the Lord, the Most High God.

Some people read the story of Ruth and, I believe, misinterpret it. Ruth was not looking for a man! Her focus was on the Lord. Her mother-in-law was the one to tell Ruth the next steps. It's important for older women to teach younger ones (Titus 2:4). Naomi instructed Ruth to go to the threshing floor, where Boaz would winnow barley. Ruth was not just going to present herself in any type of way to Boaz. Naomi instructed Ruth to bathe, put on perfume, and dress in her nicest clothes. She wanted Ruth to look presentable and prepared, not like she just came out of the fields.

Ruth obeyed everything Naomi had told her to do. However, the marriage proposal by Boaz did not happen in this scenario. Boaz was a respectable and honest man. He knew there was a proper way to propose, and he wanted to do it the right way. During this time, Ruth had to wait and be patient, as instructed by Naomi.

From facing isolation and loneliness due to the death of her husband, to moving to a foreign land where no one knew her, this was all a part of God's refinement in Ruth. In due time, God's perfect plan for Ruth came to fruition with the marriage of Boaz and the birth of Obed (the grandfather of King David). This was a picture of God's divine plan to bring His son, Jesus Christ, through the lineage of Boaz and Ruth. What a beautiful example of refinement!

Like Ruth, and Job, David and Esther, our current situations and hurdles might well be the indicators of God's refinement process toward a victorious future!

CHAPTER 2: EXTRACTION

Taking out by force

E

xtraction is the action of taking or pulling out something, especially using effort or force. With God as the Refiner, I will take you through a journey of my extraction process. As we go down this journey, consider and reflect on how God has refined you. What has He done in your life to make this possible? How and what did it take to bring you to where you are today, in Him? What other element of extraction is still needed?

Remember that we will never fully arrive at complete refinement until heaven. There is and will always be some type of extraction in each of us. Mine may look different from yours, but it is still a process. It's the pressing and crushing, making you new and fine as pure gold. The end result is pure and holy, just as Christ. That is God working in and through you, not you yourself. Thanking Him for being there throughout the process. It is a beautiful thing indeed.

"...What comes out of a person is not what defiles them. For it is from within, out of a person's heart, that evil thoughts come - sexual immorality, theft, murder, adultery, greed, malice, deceit, lewdness, envy, slander, arrogance and folly. All these evils come from inside and defile a person..."

(Mark 7:20-23 NIV)

As previously mentioned, in order for gold to be refined, it has to go through the process of being removed from unwanted impurities. There are various methods of this extraction process, but the primary goal is to remove the substance of interest from unwanted impurities. The extraction of sexual immorality, perversion, unforgiveness, anger, and so much more. The extraction process is never easy and requires placing the desired substance in extremely uncomfortable environments, in order for the impurities to be removed.

Let me tell you that many of the environments God allowed me to go through were indeed uncomfortable, to say the least—yet necessary. I didn't realize it at the time, but He was refining me. I just felt as though I was being punished—likely for some sort of wrongdoing on my part. Little did I know, God allowed these tests and trials in my life to draw me closer to Him.

CHAPTER 2: EXTRACTION

> *"I was clueless about what I was getting myself
> into during my adolescent years."*

I vividly recall my extraction process. It all began in undergraduate school at Columbus State University, in Columbus, Georgia. I was a freshman. My first take on adulthood. Life was perfect as I knew it. I had friends, a boyfriend, and a carefree life. It appeared everything was going well. Until it all came crumbling down. Let me back up and talk about my life, prior to this point.

I grew up in the inner city of Boston. My mom and dad divorced when I was about four years old. I never knew how it was to have my father in the house. It was mainly my mom, brother, and I. Although I have an older brother, about ten years apart in age, he never lived with us permanently. He also has a different father from my brother and me.

I was raised in the church. It was a very strict apostolic church in Roxbury, Massachusetts. I would spend most of my childhood in church, outside of school, and visiting family. On Sundays, we would be there from morning until noon. Often, there would be food upstairs for us to eat. The mothers of the church would make the best fried chicken and sweet potato pies I have ever had in my life! There were many strict rules and regulations from the church that were a part of my everyday life. I could not wear pants as a female or celebrate any major holidays, except Thanksgiving and our birthdays. There was even a time when my mom had me in Ballet but quickly took me out because the church was against my wearing a leotard. I didn't understand it all at the time. As a child, who would? All you wanted to do was have fun and enjoy your life.

I heard about Jesus but didn't really know who He was. All I knew was the shouting and dancing at church and the outward appearance of being a 'good Christian;' however, I never had a change of heart. I didn't understand much at this point, not even the true Gospel of Jesus Christ. Of course, I knew He died on the cross. But what did that mean? What did that look like? Why did He do it? I didn't truly understand love because it was not tangible in my 'now' reality.

Sometimes my father came around; it was love at first sight! The love I was hoping and longing for. I was indeed a daddy's girl. I loved him so much! However, there were moments of disappointment, isolation, and resentment with him. One day, when I was little; I was waiting by the window for my dad to show up. He mentioned he would stop by to pick up my brother and me. After waiting by the window for hours, I realized, once dusk hit, that he would not be coming. As I grew older, these moments would linger in my mind and create an image of my dad, or at least who I thought he was. Since I never really had that father-daughter relationship growing up, my dad was a mystery to me. I wanted to know more about him. As the disappointments grew, the mystery only became a facade to the reality of who he was. These were the moments and times that hurt the most.

So, with that came abandonment issues and rejection. My not feeling good enough for a man to love me. Infinite times, I would replace this with love from a boy I liked in school or even a 'mystery man' I met in different parts of my life growing up. One time in middle school, people asked my well-known crush why he didn't like me. The next thing he said, which I dreaded to hear, was *"Because she's ugly..."* I was not only embarrassed; I was deeply hurt. I never really had a man tell me I was beautiful. So, for some of the first words about my appearance from any man or boy were to say I was ugly really struck a nerve in me.

From then on, I would accept the fact that I wasn't as pretty as the other girls in my class. I wasn't a 'pretty girl' to be sought after by other boys in my school. There were many other instances growing up of my encounter with boys that really turned into them being that 'mystery man or boy.' Situations where I didn't know it but I really was searching for the fulfillment of my own father in my life. I recall spending one summer at my grandparents' house. Normally, my mom would place us in summer camp or Vacation Bible School, but for some reason, my brother and I stayed at my grandparents' house more than usual this summer. I was not even thirteen but I remember my cousins and I playing cards (mostly Spades) and hanging out on my grandparents' porch.

My grandparents didn't stay in the best of neighborhoods—but not the worst either, if I could remember correctly. Lots of gang violence and drugs; however, it was safe enough for all of us to stay out on the front porch or walk to the corner store alone. Having not much to do, going to the corner store and playground was the highlight of the day. One time at the playground, I met this boy. He seemed to take an interest in me. Every time I came to the playground with my cousin, he and I would sit on the seesaw to talk. He called me his 'girlfriend' and told me he was in a gang—but I did not know what all of that even meant. I knew it wasn't the best idea to talk to him, so I ensured no one knew about him. After a few 'playground' meetups, I would never see him again. I can't remember why, but I believe that God removed him from my life for a reason.

Another encounter was with a store clerk from the corner store near my house. My mom would send us to this corner store to buy groceries. He passed me a note at the register asking me if I would be his girlfriend, with the check box "yes" or "no." A few days later, I returned to the store with my checked response of "yes." This situation was even more of a 'mystery' type of relationship, as our only communication was through the notes we would pass when I came into the store. I never even heard him talk. It got to the point where I was tired of writing notes and decided to 'break up' with him—through a note.

These experiences affected how I perceived boys and even men, in my limited understanding as a child. I didn't know who I was and how to interact much with the opposite sex. The perception of a man was from the absence of a father in the home. I didn't realize it at the time, but I was projecting my thoughts and feelings of who I wanted a man to be onto a young boy who barely even knew who he was himself.

I was exposed to pornography at a very young age. It was being watched in the same room that I was in. Although I wasn't directly watching and had my back turned away, the spirit of lust crept in. With that, it opened the door to sexual perversion and same-sex attraction. I became addicted to watching sex scenes from different movies. Being that my mom was strict with what we could watch, I had limited exposure to rated R movies containing sex scenes. So, this limited the perversion to my imagination. There was a time when watching a TV show, I even kissed the screen, pretending I was kissing one of the actresses. With this perversion came me thinking that I could be a boy or a girl. I had the option to change genders. I don't know where or how this thought started. No one ever told me I could or could not switch genders—however, it was another deception that I was exposed to through pornography and sexual perversion.

Gender confusion opened the door to child-on-child same-sex abuse. We barely even knew what we were doing. All I knew was that it was physically satisfying. There was a moment I believe we got caught, but I couldn't recall the punishment. Nor did anyone explain to us that what we were doing was wrong. I may have gotten a beating for this—but again, I cannot recall the events.

Speaking of beatings, yes, I was physically and verbally abused at home as a child. It's one thing to have someone you barely know call you names, but another thing to hear from the mouth of someone you think you can trust—specifically my mother. There were times my mother called me names I would rather not repeat. This hurt and lingered more than the physical beatings. There's a saying that sticks and stones can break my bones, but words can never hurt me. That's just not true—words do hurt—and may even last longer than physical wounds. One time, my mother called me a name, and my auntie turned and looked at me, telling me I was so beautiful. That really stayed with me. However, it couldn't replace the deep hurt and pain of verbal abuse by my mother. This opened the door further to feelings of rejection and low self-esteem.

I never was able to develop any solid relationships with other people around my age. The only person I could remember being the closest to is my brother. He is two years older than me, and we have the same mother and father. At first, we started going to the same school. If there was one thing my brother took seriously—that was to protect his little sister (well, in public, at least).

There was a time in second grade after school, as I was walking to the bus, a boy knocked my books down to the ground while he was walking by me. When he saw that all my books were on the ground, the boy turned and laughed. My brother saw what had transpired and immediately reacted. He ran onto the bus and started beating up the boy. I wasn't on the bus at the time to fully view, but I could see my brother on top of the boy, swinging his arms to hit him.

Oftentimes, while my mom was not home, my brother and I would build forts and climb all over the house. We would be sure to clean and place everything back where it was before my mother came home (we knew better). We had our own 'sibling' language, inside jokes, and even ate paper together (don't even ask why). He would practice wrestling movies on me, such as The Stone-Cold Stunner—which was likely dangerous, considering how skinny and fragile I was as a child. He could have easily hurt me. There was one time he ended up giving me a black eye while play fighting. My brother knew he could only do this with me when my mom wasn't home, being that while she was home, she would ensure my brother wouldn't play rough with me.

One time, my mother told my brother that he would get a whooping along with me, because I forgot to wash the dishes. My brother thought it was unfair, so he planned to run away. Being the little sister, and always wanting to be around my brother, I thought I would run away too! It only made sense. We planned it out—to not eat our lunch so we would have something for the journey after school. However, I was hungry during lunchtime and ate mine. We took the long journey after school of running away…to our grandparents' house. My oldest brother, who was living there at the time, opened the door—and that was the end of our mini runaway adventure.

I remember making it back home after my grandfather dropped my brother and me off. I thought we would get in more trouble than originally planned. Thankfully, nothing happened. My mom was likely just relieved that we were okay. While my brother was asleep, my mom asked me if it was my brother's idea to run away, and I whipped out a quick *"yes."* Ha! I definitely threw him under the bus at that moment.

I will never forget those moments of growing up with my brother. However, as my brother got older, he started getting into trouble and doing many things that, as a child, I didn't understand. He was a child himself. Looking back, I understood it was a way for him to cope with not having our father in the home.

For as long as I can remember, we never stayed in the same school. We would switch schools for one reason or the other, but mainly because my brother was getting into trouble. This was similar to how my mom grew up. She fought her way through her early years of school. I have stories piled up of how my mom beat up some girl or even boy. To say the least, my brother took after her with the fighting. With that came the consequences of him getting into trouble, and my mom, being the protector she is, defending my brother and deciding for both of us to change schools. It's not that she thought he was innocent, but my mother wanted both of us to have a chance at achieving our greatest potential.

For my brother, school was his least favorite thing in life. As for me, I loved school. I enjoyed learning. In elementary school, I would be the first to finish my schoolwork, then turn around and talk to my classmate behind me. This would get me into trouble, as I was disturbing other classmates in finishing their work and would often lead to me getting a 'C' in conduct on my report card, with all other A's and B's. However, the ever-shifting environments and schools prevented me from developing a solid foundation of friendships. I didn't understand it as a child, but as I grew older, I realized this was the root of instability in my life.

The changing environments in my childhood made it difficult for me to develop solid friendships and relationships with others. Even to this day, I have been one to take risks and move somewhere, lacking solid roots anywhere in particular. Thank God for His grace and for showing me recently how to be stable and deeply rooted where I am.

One thing my mom made sure of was that I received a good education. She wanted me to succeed in life academically. She had me apply to a private school in Brookline, MA. This school was on the outskirts of Boston, far from where we were currently living. During my middle school years and beyond, this school had a major influence on my life, even to this day. I went on my first camping trip, learned Spanish, developed in various sports, and much more. From sixth through most of ninth grade, I was at this predominantly Jewish private school, attending a fair amount of Bar and Bat Mitzvahs. Compared to the other girls, I was not the most popular but also not the most nerdy/unpopular. I was average in popularity, played many sports, and developed a skill for being a soccer goalie. Things were going well.

For the first time, life was stable. I started gaining more friends as I got to know others. As new people came into the school, it was the first time I wasn't a newbie. It felt good! Like a sense of belonging.

Then, one day, my mom decided she wanted us to move to Georgia. A year prior to this, my mom moved down there for a job. During that time, my aunt and two younger cousins moved in with my brother and I. Living with my aunt was a major change from living with my mom. She would bake chocolate chip cookies from scratch; that were so good! If there was ever an issue or she was upset, she would talk to us and share her frustrations without raising her voice or calling us out of our names. It was definitely a change from what we were used to.

When my mom came back to Boston after being away for some time, I had no idea she planned on moving us down to Georgia with her. I was just finishing ninth grade. Moving to the South was something I never wanted, as I would be away from family, friends, and all I ever knew. Building relationships was already difficult, and now I had to move and build new ones. I thought it was unfair and selfish on my mother's part. But as a child, you have no say in the matter. So, just like that, we moved.

We stayed in a one-bedroom apartment in Norcross, GA. I hated it, to say the least. Not only was I moving to a foreign land, but I also had to share my privacy with my mom and brother. In Boston, I had my own room, my own privacy, and my sense of being. Growing into adolescence, I needed this time to myself. In addition, I now had to transition into a public school, starting over again in building relationships. I didn't even know how or where to begin.

Public school exposed me to many new things that I never knew existed while in private school in Boston. One of the many things was being in a relationship with the opposite sex. In private school, there were a limited number of guys I would be interested in, and vice versa. Also, extracurricular activities, such as basketball and soccer, took up most of my downtime. I never knew how it felt to be desired and to desire someone, especially in a physical or sexual manner. Yes, there were the playground and store clerk 'boyfriends'—but these didn't really count.

I ended up falling for the first guy who looked my way and paid me any mind (and I liked too). Let's call him *JJ*. JJ rarely came to school, and when he did, he would only hang out in the hallways. We mainly got to know each other through gatherings outside of school—mostly at parties. It didn't take long for me to fall head over heels in lust with him and, shortly after, physical encounters with one another. Although I did not have sex with him, I did not know that there were other ways to contract a sexually transmitted disease (STD). Soon after, I started itching and had a vaginal discharge—something I never had before. I ignored it and kept on going with my life. I didn't tell anyone about it, but I knew something was off. So, I handled it myself with over-the-counter products.

I remember my mom one day taking me to the doctor. She didn't tell me why, but she knew something was wrong with me. Little did I know that the appointment about to happen was an intervention session. Medical Edition. I looked at the doctor with a straight face, who seemed like a parent towards me himself, and said, *"I am not having sex..."* which was partially true. But although I wasn't having sexual intercourse at the time, there were other encounters that were causing some issues. I wished I had gotten that check-up that day. Unfortunately, it didn't happen. We will talk about this more later.

"Do not be deceived: Bad company ruins
good morals..." (1 Corinthians 15:33 ESV)

Fast forward to my graduating high school and leaving for college. It was time for me to officially become an adult. My freshman year of college was one of the best years of my young adult life that I could remember, or so I thought. I was finally free to move outside of my mother's house—and boy, was I ready! There were too many rules and regulations that I didn't want to abide by. I thought I knew and understood the world at the prime age of eighteen.

However, what I really wanted was to run away. Run away from the hurt of not having my father in my home. Run away from the fact my brother, whom I was closest to, had been acting out in school and eventually ended up in and out of jail most of my young adult life. It was a sad reality to take in, that he would never make it to any major events in my life. Not that I held this against him, but this was something that made me feel isolated from him and all the rest of my family. He was my best friend growing up.

As life may have it, my brother was dealing with his own struggles and disappointments and handled it the way he knew best. These times were difficult for me, as I missed my brother and the solid relationship we had built. Towards the end of my high school years, I would end up visiting him in a juvenile detention center.

Driving down to Columbus, GA, to move to a city of the unknown, where people didn't know me, and I didn't know others, was a great opportunity to start over and finally be free! However, I didn't expect the stress of living on my own to be so great. Attempting to go to school and balancing the responsibilities of adulthood really was something. I don't think any eighteen-year-old can ever expect how it will be to live on their own right away. It takes the highs and the lows.

> *"I thought they were envious of me and my boyfriend."*

One thing I could remember about Columbus, GA, it was the 'country!' Even more 'country' and 'southern' than Atlanta—and VERY boring. Outside of hanging out and partying, there was nothing to do. I took a position at Publix as a cashier to help with minor bills, as I had previously worked with Publix throughout high school in Norcross, GA. Working there would give me a little extra change I could use for minor living expenses such as gas and groceries. Most of my income, however, was through student loans. I always took out the maximum amount of loans. This would help sustain me. I didn't realize at the time, that these would have to be paid back! During my first year of college, my focus was not on school…I wanted to live a life of freedom. Freedom from my old self and the rules and regulations of my mother. I recall being so excited to leave her house.

As a freshman, they required that students stay on campus; however, because the dorms were full, I had the luxury of staying off campus with a roommate. That required my needing transportation to get around. I moved down the street from campus. My mother knew that I needed a vehicle, and she agreed to give me hers. For my mom, that was a huge sacrifice. Something that, as a college student, I didn't immediately recognize and even took for granted.

My mom chose to use public transportation, to ensure I had a vehicle. Not just any public transportation, but that in the south, which was subpar from many northern states' public transportation. I do not recall saying *"thank you"* to her for doing this, although I'm pretty sure I did. Either way, my focus was on leaving. And with that, I packed up my mother's old white Nissan Altima and headed down to Columbus. Little did I know there would be many memories with that car, some more tragic than others.

I remember going out one night and meeting this guy who automatically caught my attention. Let's call him *CJ*. CJ had this thick black curly hair, silky as can be, light-skinned, and a face chiseled and fine. I thought it was indeed 'love' at first sight. I made the first move and gave him my number. I didn't say a thing to him. I just gave him my number and walked away. I had no clue he would actually call me. That was the beginning of a rocky relationship that would take years to heal from.

We ended up dating and having sex, and he even made me his 'girl.' My first real boyfriend. But what did that even mean? I knew I enjoyed our sexual encounters, but was there anything else? We moved fast in the relationship, me meeting his family and him meeting some of mine. But I wasn't ready for a relationship, and neither was he. We were young, foolish, and in lust.

CJ introduced me to marijuana. I had only one previous encounter with marijuana before with some co-workers from Publix, and at the time, I did not get 'high.' This time, however, was different. Each time we would smoke, we would end up having sex. I started becoming unknowingly addicted to both...more so the high during sex than anything. It made sex that much more pleasurable. It got to a point with me asking for us to smoke prior to having sex. I was in over my head and going down a dark path; I couldn't see my way out.

Eventually, our relationship took a turn for the worse, with no regard or respect for each other. We eventually broke up. For reasons he blamed me. Remember my mentioning the STD I contracted in high school? Well, it never completely cleared up. My boyfriend accused me of giving him an STD. I was devastated. I ended up going to a clinic to get treatment. However, the pain of the breakup lingered.

As a result, I headed down a very dark path that I never knew I could go. I thought I would easily get over him, but something yearned for and desired him so much. I felt like I was in love and didn't know how to rid myself of it. At some point, I even attempted to end my own life. I thought this would rid me of the hurt and guilt caused by the breakup. I thought the easiest way would be hanging myself, so I attempted to do so by wrapping a belt around my bathroom shower rod. That turned out to be a failed attempt. Even worse, it left a mark on my neck. At some point, people thought this mark was a hickey. Of course, I would not dare tell anyone the truth about the mark.

Soon, my ex started calling me again. I guess he was just as tied spiritually to me as I was to him. However, I knew he was no good. We eventually got back together. Then, we broke up again. Then back together. Then broke up again. It was a never-ending roller coaster ride that needed to end immediately! I recall one time being at his parents' house, and we got into an argument. It was silly looking back, but I was so immature, insecure, and foolish. It was Valentine's Day, and we were going to Macon, GA, for a comedy show. We got into our usual argument; however, this time, I hit him. I couldn't believe myself and how far things had gone. I was just waiting for his reaction. He took his time to ponder, think about it, walked up to me, and slapped me in the face. My heart hurt more than the hit. I knew we had lost respect for each other.

During this rocky relationship, I became jealous, controlling, and possessive. I didn't want him to be around anyone else—especially females. Even though CJ had friends, I was in a very low space in life and struggled with isolation. I did not have many friends, and truthfully, my time was occupied with making him my god. And to be honest, a man is a terrible god.

There was a time when he came over, and he was conversing with my roommate and her friends. The thing about this situation was that my roommate and I didn't get along. Neither did I get along with her friends. Ironically, we used to all be friends and hang out together. But the obsession with my boyfriend took over, and I didn't value having anyone in my life except for him. So, when he spoke with them, I immediately became jealous. When we made it to my room, I scolded him out loud where they could hear me saying everything—including the fact that I didn't like them. This turned into a vicious trap of the devil. A few hours later, the girls confronted me while I was leaving my room to throw away some trash. One girl hit me on the side of my temple, and they then attempted to jump me. I couldn't believe what was happening. To think these girls used to be my friends…it definitely hurt.

Although we grew apart, he went his way, and I went mine; there was still the hurt and emotional heartbreak that lingered on. The only way I knew how to fix things, in my fleshly way of thinking, was to have sex—and that I did. This was the point I can say I was the most promiscuous I had ever been in my life. I wanted to get rid of the hurt, anger, and disappointment of not being with the one I really wanted to be with. I didn't know how to cope any other way.

Despite the fact that I grew up in the church, I never really thought about going to God. It wasn't in the forefront of my mind at the time. I knew the traditions of the church without the understanding of a relationship with the one and true living God. However, I knew that what I was doing was wrong—and the more I continued, the deeper my downfall would be. But I did not know how to get out of the mess. I was digging myself deeper and deeper into fornication, sexual immorality, drugs, and alcohol. In no time, I soon found something that could soothe me in addition to fornication.

Drinking was my way out of reality. I would convince myself that it wasn't an addiction, since I was only a social drinker, just when I went out to parties. Then, I realized more and more how dependent I would become on alcohol. It was my drug of choice for boldness, fearlessness, and having a good time. One time, on New Year's Eve, I went out with an old high school friend. He rented a limousine, and we drove through downtown Atlanta. I don't recall all the details of that night, but I remember opening the limousine door and screaming out, *"Happy New Year!"* At one point, when I screamed out Happy New Year, a police officer on a bike saw me. As if it were slow motion, I could read his lips telling me, *"Close the door."* I thought it was funny at the time, but in fact, it was stupid and incredibly dangerous.

Towards the end of the night, I was so drunk that as we were leaving downtown, I headed back to the limo and hit my head on the door. The next morning, I woke up with an enormous lump on my forehead. This was just one example of many encounters I would have with alcohol.

> *"My heart was filled with indignation; I didn't believe I deserved that type of treatment."*

There was a co-worker of mine who always wore long skirts. It reminded me of my growing up in church and having to always wear skirts. One day, I asked her what church she went to, and started attending her church in Phenix City, Alabama. This was a very important time in my life, where I was learning and getting to know God on my own. Prior to this, God had woken me up to the realization of life being too short, with me getting into a five-car accident.

Remember the white Nissan Altima I previously mentioned my mom giving me before I left for college? Well, there was a time I was driving towards my college campus. It was dusk. While attempting to make a left turn, an oncoming car hit me head-on. The car passed around and hit two other cars, and I hit a car behind me, before landing in the bushes on the property of an Applebee's restaurant. I immediately got out of the car, thinking it would explode. My face was burning, which I later found was because of the gunpowder from the airbag. I thought I had a broken jaw or something worse. To this day, I could not remember seeing that oncoming car. However, it was dusk, and the driver admitted they didn't have their headlights on—not to mention the car being black.

During the accident, as the car was spinning, pictures of my life flashed in my mind, and all I could remember saying was, *"Oh God, oh God!"* Coming out of the accident with just a busted lip and bruised chin, I knew more than ever that life was short, and it could be taken away at any moment! Hence, my desire to find a church.

At the beginning of attending the church in Phenix City, I remember a time when the pastor mentioned she threw all her worldly CDs out the window when she came to Christ. I thought to myself, *"I could never do that…"* Although I was going to church, I would leave out of the church and turn back on Rhianna, Beyonce, or Maria Carey.

I was wearing the long skirts again and attempting to be 'good' in my own efforts, but my heart was still not completely there. I was searching and seeking to do things in my own strength. I could remember it being like this at my childhood church in Boston, so I never thought there was anything wrong with what I was doing. 'Churchianity' is what I called it. Doing 'good' things for the Lord, but not having a heart posture change. The Bible says, our righteousness is but filthy rags (Isaiah 64:6). However, God was patient with me during this part of my extraction process. Looking back, I am grateful for this church. Although not perfect on its own, it was the Oasis in the desert that I was looking for and that God was leading me towards.

Soon, the parties were getting old. I was ready to move on to what brought me to school in the first place—my career. I originally desired to become a pediatrician (being that I had a pediatrician when I was younger that I absolutely admired). However, I focused on finishing my required courses and decided to pursue pharmacy school. My college advisor at the time told me that I would never be a pharmacist with the grades I had.

Due to my first two years of partying and bad relationships, my grades suffered, especially chemistry. I tried to speak with the professor who failed me about changing my grade, but with a smile, he said, *"No."* I knew my chemistry professor had done the right thing by not changing my grade. However, I also knew it would affect my GPA and remain on my record, possibly preventing me from getting into pharmacy school. As a result, I had to repeat the course. That taught me a hard lesson about life and its consequences. I am grateful to my chemistry professor for standing his ground and making me retake the course. It was God's extraction at work, instilling in me academic responsibility, discipline, and structure that would help to refine my future.

After graduating from undergrad, I took some time off and moved back to Atlanta. This was a year of what I would call 'backsliding.' I started going out to parties/clubs and fornicating again. This time, I was of age and could go into any club I desired. Working as a technician at a local Publix pharmacy, I knew I needed change, but did not know how to go about the process.

One day, I received a text from an old friend from undergrad. We will call her NC. NC was in pharmacy school and asked me what I was doing with my life. She knew I had the desire to go to pharmacy school as well. That sparked something in me. I knew that I wouldn't want to be a technician all my life. I needed to go after that 'Pursuit of Happiness.' Well, so I thought. I envisioned having a good career as the pursuit of happiness. Once I became a pharmacist, all my cares and problems would go away. Little did I know, I was still in the early stages of my refinement process.

Applying to pharmacy school was one of the most difficult things that I had ever done. Not only was I not a good standardized test taker, I didn't have the most competitive GPA. You can say I wasn't 'qualified.' But God! I remembered another girl and myself studying together for the pharmacy entrance exam, PHORCAS. I took the exam at least twice, only to find out how uncompetitive my score would be. Ironically,

I would score high or above average on the writing portion but not the multiple-choice sections. I honestly felt so discouraged. There was a time when NC invited me to come down and visit the school she was attending in Florida. It was a historically black college or university (HBCU), and fortunately, it did not require a standardized test for me to get in.

Visiting the school, I met a faculty member who, I believe, was God-sent. Let's call her *Mrs. G.* I went up to the office to introduce myself to her, as directed by my friend. Mrs. G looked at me puzzled and retorted, *"You came all the way here, from Georgia, to say hi?"*

I nodded an innocent yet clueless *"Yes."*

"Step into my office," she replied. As I went into her office and sat down, she looked over my records. After a brief silence, she said, *"Well, all I can say is that you are qualified."*

Not long after, I would get the acceptance letter I had been desiring. God opened a door that no man could shut. With that, I got into pharmacy school!

Pharmacy school exposed the deeper, hidden things in my heart that needed to be revealed. At first, I didn't realize this. I was so focused on becoming a pharmacist and starting a new life with new friends—something I was used to doing throughout life. Making friends was easy, being that I was sociable and outgoing. However, keeping them was the tough part. That meant they had to get to know me. Not just on the surface, but the real me. Something I didn't even fully know of myself. So, instead of friends, I made associates. Classmates. They had their own issues and eventually fell away. Either through misunderstandings or lack of communication, I soon lost these 'associates.' I jumped from one friend group to another.

A downward spiral of the realities of my past, coming to a head. I couldn't deny or blame anyone—the common denominator was me. Thankfully, God showed me a group of classmates who, until this day, would become lifelong friends—the *Jamaica Krew*. During pharmacy school, we planned a trip to Jamaica that allowed me a chance to really see how God can place people in my life to love me, no matter what I did or said.

During that trip to Jamaica, there was a time in the club I couldn't find any of them. I panicked, thinking they had left me. Being in Jamaica all alone, as a single female, was a scary thought. Not even five minutes later, they would appear. One of them, I will call her *T. Mac*, appeared, and I immediately started to yell, *"Where were you!?"* She looked at me as though I had gone mad. She explained that she went to the restroom. I was so upset with everyone for a good fifteen minutes. Soon, another friend, whom I will call *Lady D*, had a brother who was with us and was able to calm me down. Looking back, I acted like a madwoman. Not thinking rationally and having those past fears of rejection and abandonment festering in my mind. All the while, these were true friends—and even to this day, I can call my genuine friends who care about me.

The extraction process really came to a head when I hit rock bottom. One summer night, I went out with my roommate. Let's call her *MJ*. MJ was a fairly new roommate, and I had never hung out with her before. That night, I didn't want to hang out—but I didn't know or understand why. As I was getting dressed, I stood in my bedroom full mirror, staring at myself and thinking, *"Why do I not feel like going out tonight?"* Then, this other thought came to mind, *"You only live once (YOLO)."*

I didn't realize it then, but I know now that the second thought was from the enemy. The word of God says that the thief [aka Satan] comes to steal, kill, and destroy and that Jesus has come that we may have life and life to the fullest (John 10:10). If I had only known this would be one of the worst decisions in my life. Now, looking back, if I had known even a little of the Word of God, I would have stayed home that night. However, I didn't.

Before we went to the club, MJ wanted to stop by her friend's house. He made us a drink in a Styrofoam cup. To this day, I have no idea what was in that cup. One thing I did know was, immediately after drinking what he made, I was drunk.

Arriving at the club, I recalled it being one of the most promiscuous, perverse, and dark nights of my life. There was a guy I knew at the time I was dancing with. Out of nowhere, a random girl bumped into me and asked me if I was gay, and we started dancing together with him. There was such a dark and lustful presence around us. I knew it stunk in God's nostrils. But that was just the beginning of what the enemy had in store for that night. After leaving the club, I headed to the parking lot, with MJ, to leave. I did not know what was about to transpire. As I was driving, I nicked a car in the parking lot. The girl whose car I nicked came out, yelling at us. MJ started yelling back at her. While they were arguing, I interjected to help defend my roommate, and the girl hit me in the face.

I was in disbelief. How did the night come to all of this? I walked away, knowing that if I hit her back, I would go to jail. Soon, the police arrived. I knew things were about to get worse. As I was waiting in the car for the police to come to me, a random guy walked by and stopped at my window, looking to see who was around; he told me it wasn't looking good for me and that I should leave. Frantic, I tried to drive off, but the police blocked me from getting out of the parking lot. Soon, the police came over and started asking me questions. It was too late. They already had a picture of the situation in their minds. I was asked to do a sobriety test. During the sobriety test, I thought to myself, *"It will all be over soon...Just pass this test, and they will let you go..."* That didn't happen.

Next, an officer asked me to turn around and place my hands behind my back. I didn't realize that they were arresting me until they placed the handcuffs on me. I was in utter shock at what was happening. While riding in the back of the police vehicle, I pleaded with the officer, asking them to please not take me to jail. It was a plea from deep within. A cry of desperation. I ended up in the holding cell in front of the jail. At first, there were other females there to talk to. However, soon, they were gone. I faced the sobering reality of what had transpired that night.

At some point, while in the holding cell, jail inmates lined up outside. The holding cell had a big glass window that everyone could look through and see me sitting there. One of the girls in line looked at me with a threatening look. Although she was not verbally talking to me, I could tell in her eyes that she was thinking, *"When you get back there, you're mine..."* I was terrified of the thought of going back into the actual jail with the other jail inmates. Thankfully, I didn't. Even in that instance, God protected me. In the early morning, they allowed me to make two phone calls. One was to my friend,

NC, and the other to my mother. Around the time I made the call to my mother, it occurred to me it was Mother's Day. I officially hit a new kind of rock bottom. I thought to myself, *"How did I get here?"*

After being released from jail that day, I felt deep self-hatred and guilt for what I had done; I couldn't understand where I went wrong. I didn't know how to rid myself of this pain. I soon found myself at the house of a guy I was talking to at the time. There's a saying in the Bible that bad company corrupts good character (1 Corinthians 15:33), and that indeed was the case here. The guy I was talking to was no good. He even had a DUI. I didn't realize it then, but surrounding myself with someone like him opened demonic realms and principalities. What was worse, I didn't know how to fight in the spiritual realm against these principalities.

I knew there had to be some major changes in my life. But what was I to do? Who was I to turn to? Soon, I attended church again. This time, it was not in a 'Churchianity' type of way, but more so that I needed to rid myself of this guilt and shame. I needed someone to save me from the mess of who I was. I needed Christ.

CHAPTER 3: ISOLATION

Separation to obtain purity

I solation is the process of separation of one substance from another to obtain a pure or uncontaminated state. A refinery requires a substance to be isolated in order to be completely purged. This is a requirement! There is no way to be completely refined without isolation. Isolation involves disconnecting or separation from other things to focus on the primary concern: YOU! For example, when refining gold, there is a necessary step to separate the gold from all other impurities. It needs to be isolated using the extraction process (e.g., fire), in order to be purified and ultimately refined to its final state. Without removing impurities, through isolation, there is no true refinement.

Many parts of the Scripture show that even Jesus, a perfect man, desired to isolate Himself. This was necessary in order for Him to hear from the Father.

CHAPTER 3: ISOLATION

"After He had sent crowds away, He went up on a mountain by Himself to pray, and when it was evening, He was there alone..." (Matthew 14:23 NASB)

"Very early in the morning, while it was still dark, Jesus got up, left the house and went off to a solitary place, where He prayed..." (Mark 1:35 NIV)

Reflecting on my life, I realized some things needed to go. I had to be isolated from people, situations, and/or circumstances that were connected to the impurities. In this case, sin. As you may have recognized in my extraction process, sin was running rampant in my life. Sexual promiscuity, alcohol, and drugs were just the surface. There were deep issues that needed to be uprooted.

The isolation process allowed me to dig deeper and find those hard-to-reach areas in me that needed refinement. The Word of God says, *"Our hearts are deceitful and desperately wicked, who can know it? God knows our hearts..."* (Jeremiah 17:9-10). He created us. He knows that if we walk in the flesh, we will only bring satisfaction to our flesh. This is why we need to pray, fast, and read His word.

> *"Man may fail me,*
> *but God never fails!"*

Isolation involved me removing certain friend groups. During my extraction process, I saw how people who I thought were my friends, were not. The situation with the girls who jumped me over a conversation with my ex-boyfriend, CJ, is a good example. Even in the situation of me getting arrested, I surrounded myself with the wrong group of people: MJ, my roommate and her friend, who I rarely hung around.

As previously mentioned, the Word of God says that bad company corrupts good morals. Not that I had the most Biblical morals to begin with, but I did have standards and values instilled in me from a young age, growing up in a home of rules and regulations (although I tried to rebel against them). Sticking around groups of people with poor character and morals only had a negative impact on my life. I needed to be isolated from these things to be refined. God was continuously leading me away from people and circumstances that would have a negative influence on my life. I slowly learned it was necessary to remove certain people from my inner circle, even those who claimed to be Christians. We will talk about this in a moment.

Before moving on, let me explain a bit more regarding having an inner circle. There is a verse in the book of Ezekiel that talks about inner and outer courts. Ezekiel 8:16 (NIV) reads, *"He then brought me into the inner court of the house of the Lord, and there at the entrance to the temple, between the porch and the altar, there were about twenty-five men..."* Although this verse is referencing the beginning of a prophetic vision of the New Jerusalem, there is more to this inner and outer court reference throughout the Bible.

In Jesus' time, the temple was divided into two unequal sections—inner and outer courts. The outer court was the largest section and open to everyone. The inner court was more special, and only certain people could enter. These two courts became a metaphor for two categories of Israelites—the Levitical Priests (Levites) versus the rest of the tribes of Israel (Exodus 27:21, Isaiah 66:21).

Similar to playing basketball (as I used to play in middle school) you would have certain parts of the court that would be easier to shoot from and make it into the basket. There would be a three-point line, which is typically more difficult to shoot from relative to the 'outer court,' and a two-point line, relative to the 'inner court.' This symbolically reflects how relationships should be. Giving associates the outer court relationships and close friends and family the inner court, with Jesus at the center.

Remember the college boyfriend, CJ, I mentioned during my extraction process? Although we dated on and off for a few years, I had to completely remove him from my life. This surprisingly took much longer than expected. There is something we call 'soul ties,' which is a spiritual attachment to someone, often due to emotional and/or physical intimacy. The Bible commands us not to be unequally yoked with unbelievers (2 Corinthians 6:14). On these terms, the Bible is referring to a spiritual *yoke*. A yoke is something you are bound or tied to, leading you in a specific direction.

I had to break the yoke of bondage to this past relationship. Over time, being physically isolated from the person helped. Thankfully, in the situation with CJ, we eventually went our separate ways for good. Often, breaking spiritual ties calls for verbally telling the person you no longer want to be 'yoked' to them. It's not that you say it in this manner, but basically, you tell them you do not want to talk to them anymore. This is something I had to do with CJ, as he came back years later trying to reconnect. After verbally telling him I did not want to see him again, I never saw or heard from him.

This may be different for you. I believe the first step is to recognize that you need to be permanently separated from the person and understand the reason why. Is there a threat to your life, sanity, or peace of mind? Is the relationship taking a toll on you spiritually, emotionally, and/or physically? Is the relationship drawing you away from God? Any of these circumstances would warrant you needing to separate from that person.

It's hard at first. But you get to the point where you're sick and tired of being sick and tired. For some people, it will take more time than others. I had to do this in many future relationships with the opposite sex, where I felt tied to the person, even without sexual involvement. Do you know you can have spiritual ties to someone without sexual intimacy? These were some of the most difficult yokes to break. More so, because I was breaking a yoke, not with just my body, but my mind, will, and emotions—or what the Bible refers to as the *heart*.

God continued to reveal to me how important it was to isolate myself from certain friend groups in order to draw closer to Him. There were people I hung around who were not the best influence on me. They were not going in the same direction that God was taking me. There was a girl I vividly remember in undergrad who was a classmate of mine. We were 'cool,' so to speak. I considered her a good friend. Although we were classmates, we eventually ended up hanging out and partying together. She was not a good influence on me. There was a time when she introduced me to *Black & Mild* cigars. I remember one day going to work and forgetting I had a *Black & Mild* in my purse from the club the previous night. The smell hit the air. It was terrible. I was too embarrassed to admit I smoked such a disgusting thing. What was hidden in the dark was coming to light—literally.

You see, in the nightclub, this was the 'cool' thing to do. I also enjoyed the light 'buzz' or high I would feel after smoking. It became addictive, although I didn't immediately notice. But at work, I realized this was not something that a woman should keep as a habit.

I immediately decided to no longer smoke. I had to recollect how I even started smoking in the first place, and it brought me back to her. Although I couldn't completely blame her. I had to own the responsibility that I was making a decision, each time I smoked. However, God continued revealing people in my life and their influence on me. What they were exposing me to. I listened. Although, many times, it took a while to grasp what God was trying to show me.

So many hurtful things have happened in past relationships. Oftentimes, I desired to get close to people, but it just wouldn't work out the way I wanted it to. There was one time I helped at the door entrance to enter a nightclub. The party was being hosted by the popularly known fraternity, the Kappas. Being Greek (part of a sorority or fraternity) was a big deal—especially with undergrads. I wanted to hang out with the 'cool' clique, which was typically connected to fraternities and sororities. As I was helping at the door of a club, there was a girl who I thought was a friend or at least an associate. Let's call her *GR*. For some reason, GR was upset with me. However, I hadn't the faintest idea or remembrance of why. She brought me a drink, while I was helping at the front. She wore the biggest grin, which I thought was a friendly smile.

After the club, there was a commotion about something. One girl, whose name was similar to mine, heard GR call her a word outside her name (a female dog). Let's call this girl *SR*. SR was upset and yelling. Everyone was crowding around to see what was going on. I realized at that moment how fast a 'friend' could change into an enemy. GR, who brought me that drink, who I thought was cool, said in front of everyone, that she was not calling SR outside of her name, but me! I was taken aback a bit. What did I ever do to her?

I had no time to think because everyone was watching. I wanted to show her she couldn't call me outside of my name either. She had to know who she was messing with. I immediately walked up and hit her in the face. This was a bad move on my part. The crazy thing was, as I hit her, I walked away with immediate regret for what I did. GR started hysterically yelling. Thank God, He protected me from getting in a full-blown fight with her or, even worse, getting jumped. Although she was yelling, it was like a wall of protection was over me, and she couldn't physically hit me. Plus, there were a few ladies, including SR, holding her back, as I watched from the corner of my eyes, walking away.

I never saw someone turn out to be the exact opposite of who they portrayed to be, all in one night! Some other women, who were supposed to be my friends there that night, took GR's side in the altercation. There were many past and future encounters that led to me being isolated from others. However, this one really hit deep.

Isolation continued at various other points of my life. I would like to fast forward to a time I was drawing closer to the Lord, and invited to a 'friend' of mine's bachelorette party. I should have known right there that this would not be a holy and sanctified gathering. Being naïve and trusting that she was a follower of Christ, based on our meeting through a women's bible study group, I decided to go. Little did I know, we were about to go downtown in the heart of Mardi Gras, in New Orleans, LA (NOLA). If you are not familiar with Mardi Gras, it is a festival that many people in NOLA, and maybe other parts of the country, celebrate. It involves parades and festivals. Many of the people who attend celebrate by drinking and partying, prior to Lent. The Bible says to not be drunk with wine—instead to be filled with the [Holy] Spirit (Ephesians 5:18). The Bible also talks about us, as believers, coming out from among unbelievers and separating ourselves from them (2 Corinthians 6:17). So, for us to be in the epicenter of debauchery and drunkenness, was not in the plan.

I know what you may be thinking, *"Girl, you should have known!"* In that situation, I didn't recognize the warning signs. I trusted my friend was who she portrayed to be. Just because someone says they are a Christian, should we not judge their fruit and character? I was hurt by the 'blind' trust of a group of women that I thought were true sisters in Christ. I placed them close to the inner court of relationships. We took a ferry to the location in what I believed to be downtown NOLA. When we got off the ferry, they wanted to take some pictures. I immediately noticed a homeless man off to the side of us.

The girls were so focused on having fun, that no one else noticed him there. He was sitting on a cardboard box. I bent down and gave him some money and told him that Jesus loved him. As we walked down the streets, we saw people yelling and partying, and they appeared to be having fun. I couldn't wait to leave. I had no desire to be there. I thought to myself, *"How did I get in this situation?"* The other girls were watching the parade and floats pass by, lifting their hands to request beads. The people on the float were throwing out beads. Out of nowhere, one large set of beads hit me right in the head. *"Ouch!"* I yelled. But no one heard or even cared to listen.

Towards the end of the night, the girls still wanted to hang out. I thought to myself, *"What is this? Why would you all want to be out amongst this type of life?"* I was confused and alone. It took a turn when they were all planning to go to a party afterward. I knew I had no choice but to separate myself. I had no car. My phone was about to die. It was rainy and cold. Late at night...and to top it off, I did not know where I was.

I somehow managed to find a corner store. From there, I called a friend of mine who lived in the area. I was heartbroken by the situation. To think that I called these women my friends. I knew they thought that I ruined their fun. However, I had to learn to forgive and move on from that situation. Even more, I had to trust God and know that there was a reason He was separating me from them.

Over the years, I have recognized that being around ungodly people can have a major impact, and quickly. If I was around someone or a group of people who were always gossiping and slandering others, I soon did the same. If around those who were discontent and always speaking about marriage and relationships, I too thought the same way. I realized that when surrounded by ungodly people, there was often a spirit of discontentment and depression that followed. Without knowing, this would lead me down a state of isolating myself from God. Thank God, that after recognizing this routine of an emotional rollercoaster relationship with Him, I became intentional about removing anything or anyone that would make it harder to build that relationship deeper in intimacy with Christ. He would soon be that centered relationship I was yearning for.

Another part of my isolation process was material things—more specifically, television (TV) shows. There was so much impurity! During my adolescent and college years, reality TV shows were a major thing. I used to watch Bad Girls Club, Real Housewives, Real World, and many other similar shows. The women on those shows were my main source of influence—especially on Bad Girls Club.

Although it portrayed women half-naked, partying, getting drunk, being promiscuous, and quarreling, this is what I looked up to. I thought I was a 'Bad Girl' and desired to be like the women I saw on TV. I recall one time, when I had a conflict with another roommate of mine while in pharmacy school. There were about fifteen of us who went on a cruise for Spring Break. My roommate and I got into a disagreement about something so insignificant I can't even recall. I took her clothes out of her own suitcase and threw them all over the floor in the cabin. This was something I felt was 'cute' because I saw similar things done on TV.

Now, looking back, there was nothing cute about this. In fact, it was an ugly character to have. This was far from any biblical or godly woman. It was necessary that I disconnected from these shows. As the Lord was pruning and molding me, He brought up situations in my life and showed me the culprit of these issues. He showed me that, for me to become whole in Him, I had to guard my heart from these types of shows. I took the extreme route and one day donated my TV away to the Salvation Army.

Secular music was another thing that I had to separate myself from. There are certain genres of music that, even to this day, I will not listen to. Regarding music, we know who has control of the power of the air–Satan (Ephesians 2:2). He has used music in so many ways to fulfill his agenda on this earth. Why partake? Music was difficult to give up. I honestly can say this was as much a soul tie and hard to let go of as the ex-boyfriend, maybe even more.

To this day, I have old songs that randomly play in my head from worldly music I used to listen to. It can sound innocent and 'old school,' but if it's not glorifying God, why listen to it? I had to isolate myself from all impurities, including secular music. I know some of you may think differently about this one. But reflect on this for a moment: if you are a true follower of Christ, why would you listen to something that glorifies someone or something other than God? Who are you placing your hope in? Who is your god? Why can't you give it up?

Remember my mentioning the pastor from a church I started going to when I was just getting back into my relationship with Him? She mentioned she threw all her CDs out of the window when she gave her life to God. I wasn't ready to do the same. I also thought it wasn't necessary and that it didn't take all that. But it really does. It was necessary to remove this impurity from my life. I had to evaluate why I couldn't initially give it up. One thing is for certain: God patiently waited for my heart's posture to change towards Him. My desires became His desires. I saw the wickedness in the music I was listening to, even when it seemed innocent. God was revealing to me this about music.

There was a song by an artist I used to listen to. A very well-known song that would be played in the clubs, and everyone would be vibing and dancing to it. People knew this song contained underlying demonic lyrics. I soon found out other music had the same. These lyrics were intentionally placed under the radar, but they were still present. There was no denying it. The word of God says you will know them by their fruit (Matthew 7:16). The fruit of many of the artists' lives reflected their heart and who their god was. If this is the case, why did I want to listen to their music and think I would not be influenced in any way? The greatest weapon of the enemy is making people believe that he doesn't exist. That is exactly the case with secular music. Denying that many of the artists and songs they produce are spiritually dangerous to listen to. There is a battle for our souls in the spiritual realm. Why give the enemy an open door to wreak havoc?

I now listen to only gospel/Christian music. Now and then, a song may pop up when I am on a Lyft or Uber ride, working out at the gym, or some other random place. I have realized how sensitive I am now to music. I can hear the wickedness in the songs. How the enemy makes it so sly and easy. Desensitizing us to his plans. I honestly believe the most difficult area for many Christians is allowing God to completely refine this area. Not that we do not want to, but because we feel it's not necessarily needed.

The Word of God makes it clear to guard your heart, because out of it flows the issues of life (Proverbs 4:23). When talking about the heart in this context, it is our mind, will, and emotions. To guard your heart is to protect it from anything or anyone that can interfere and take control of it, removing the place of God from being the center of your life. This is why it is necessary to put on the armor of God every day. In fact, let's take a look at this verse in scripture right now:

Ephesians 6:10-18 (NIV) reads:

"Finally, be strong in the Lord and in his mighty power. 11 Put on the full armor of God, so that you can take your stand against the devil's schemes. 12 For our struggle is not against flesh and blood, but against the rulers, against the authorities, against the powers of this dark world and against the spiritual forces of evil in the heavenly realms. 13 Therefore put on the full armor of God, so that when the day of evil comes, you may be able to stand your ground, and after you have done everything, to stand. 14 Stand firm then, with the belt of truth buckled around your waist, with the breastplate of righteousness in place, 15 and with your feet fitted with the readiness that comes from the gospel of peace. 16 In addition to all this, take up the shield of faith, with which you can

extinguish all the flaming arrows of the evil one. 17 Take the helmet
of salvation and the sword of the Spirit, which is the word of God.

18 And pray in the Spirit on all occasions with all kinds of prayers
and requests. With this in mind, be alert and always keep on
praying for all the Lord's people..."

There was a point in my life where I had to recite this every day in order for me to overcome strongholds. I have now memorized this scripture and use it often in the morning, in my alone time with God, to pray and dress myself for battle. When looking into this passage, we see it mentions taking on the belt of truth and the breastplate of righteousness.

When looking at how Roman soldiers used to place on their armor, they put on their belts *before* placing on their breastplates. I found that the apostle Paul did not place the order of how to put on the armor of God in vain. This is how we should dress for spiritual battle. In that order, we put on God's belt of Truth before placing on righteousness. How can we have His righteousness if we don't know His truth? His truth is found in His Word and revealed to us through the Holy Spirit.

Guarding my heart was a significant part of the isolation process. I learned that in many circumstances throughout life, it was necessary in my walk with Him. Guarding my heart did not mean placing a wall up against other people, but allowing God to be the shield of protection, through faith in Jesus Christ. It meant that I would no longer allow any thing, situation, or person to interfere with my relationship with Him. I noticed that guarding my heart was necessary in order to strengthen my relationship with Christ. There were spiritual attacks happening throughout my walk, many of them through dreams, people, and more times than not, my flesh. I've always wondered what the apostle Paul meant when he talked about a thorn in his flesh. I have realized that what the thorn is doesn't even matter all that much. Not as much as *who* relieves that thorn.

The Word of God says, *"My grace is all you need. My power works best in weakness..."* (2 Corinthians 12:9). Through many instances of guarding my heart, I realized it was irrelevant to do it in my own human efforts, if I didn't know to whom I needed to place my heart in the hands of—that is Jesus Christ. It was hard at first. During the isolation process, the only person who I could trust with my entire heart— even to this day and forever— is Jesus. Ezekiel 36:26 reads, *"And I will give you a new heart and will put a new spirit in you. I will take out your stony, stubborn heart and give you a tender, responsive heart..."*

It is God who makes the heart change. It is Him, the Great Physician of all physicians, who does the intense surgery of softening the heart towards the Gospel of Jesus Christ and His Word. It is Him that saw fit to meet me where I was—in my mess and disobedience—and see me as His, even before I knew I was His. God had to remove the things of this world from me. People, material comforts, and situations had to be removed to make this surgery successful. Proverbs 3:5 says to trust in the Lord with all thine heart; do not depend on your own understanding. God had to replace my old, rebellious, perverted mindset with a new one—HIS!

No two isolations are the same. Everyone has their own unique isolation process. God knows precisely what kind of isolation your life requires. Your isolation depends on your current condition. My isolation was the removal of every person or thing, leading me down a road to sin. This was necessary. It involved the removal of many friends and even family members that I was close to. I had to remove these things or people as idols in my life.

You see, many times, when I needed guidance or wanted emotional, spiritual, or even physical comfort, I would run to someone outside of God—whether this be my mother, a man, or anyone or anything else in between. God wanted me to Himself. He wanted me to go to Him before I did people or things. This involved fasting, praying, and seeking Him more than ever before. I had to hear from Him first. Anyone else would just be confirming what the Lord had already spoken to me through His Word or in prayer.

I want to briefly talk about fasting. This was such a vital part of my isolation process of refinery that I couldn't leave it out. To me, fasting was intentionally removing things or distractions, to hear from God and draw closer to Him. Fasting had become a way of life. It decreased my fleshly desires and increased my spiritual desires in Christ.

I isolated myself during fasts to dedicate more time to studying scripture and prayer. I used to take time off work, if possible, or even exercise. I used corporate fasts to help guide and encourage me, as led by the Holy Spirit. Most of my fasts involved me not eating; however, I had to spiritually 'build up' to this. Some of the first fasts I did involved me not getting on social media. Soon, I was able to do Daniel fasts (eating only raw fruits and vegetables).

I eventually progressed to doing no food fasts (although I would often still drink liquids). Fasting played a necessary part in developing my spiritual maturity in Christ. During this time of isolation and separation, God downloaded His Word and filled me even more with His Holy Spirit. There were revelations and breakthroughs that came about during times of fasting. The most important revelations would be Him showing me I didn't really need the cares of this world to be happy. I just needed Him! I soon removed myself from many social media pages, as I knew they were becoming an idol for me. In the beginnings of me fasting, God showed me how my diet made me sluggish and tired, and that eating healthy would help my mental, physical, and emotional health. By eating healthier, I heard more clearly from the Lord about a situation or problem. He didn't always answer how I wanted Him to, but more so the way He wanted me to see things. I learned His character and who He was, more than ever before, during the times of fasting and prayer. There are so many other aspects of fasting I would like to share, but that will need to be for another book.

Throughout the times of isolation, I still messed up. Oftentimes, it got frustrating. Yet, I saw the progress and the purpose of the process. God was faithful in my circumstances. The isolation process varied between emotional, spiritual, and physical detachment. I still interacted with others, but not on the level emotionally that I normally would. Some people's isolation may be physical removal or detachment (which, at times, mine was). There can also be spiritual detachments. You must seek God for yourself and identify the situations, things, or people you are placing before Him. Where are you finding comfort? If it is any thing, place, or person before God, you must confess your sins to Him and ask for forgiveness. He is faithful and just to forgive us and cleanse us from all unrighteousness (1 John 1:9).

> *"It was nice to know that even in my struggles, God had my back!"*

Isolation has been a recurring process in my life. Sometimes, there was no one but Christ. Where I had no one to tell the deepest and darkest concerns of my heart to, but Him. I have learned, in those seasons of my life, to consecrate myself. In these times, I was alone but *never* lonely. It was interesting. I would have some of the most joyous moments when I was going through seasons of isolation and focused just on Him. There have been points of clarity and direction in my life during these seasons. In these moments, God was teaching me, why not go to Him? He created me. He knows me far greater than I even know myself. As a single, childless, late-30s female, I am confident to say that isolation is good. In fact, it is necessary!

The isolation that I have gone through was no time to sulk (although I have started it this way plenty of times). It is time to hear from God, read His Word, and pray. I believe the

Lord isolates those He has a lot to say. He wants us to spend time with Him so that we can clearly hear what the next steps are for our assignment by Him. Isolation brought about this book. I felt the Holy Spirit urging me to write. The title of the book came before anything else. Slowly but surely, the Lord has been leading and guiding me. He even walked me through the process of planning who I should share my book journey with. Honestly, in the beginning stages of birthing the book—absolutely no one! Just Him and I. That may be hard for some...but when the Holy Spirit is leading, guiding, and prompting you, it makes it that much easier.

I thank God for the isolation season. If you look back at the people in the Bible that were called to isolation—Esther, Ruth, King David, Daniel, even Moses—these were critical times for growth and development. Going through the isolation process calls for humbleness and meekness—something I had been continually praying for in the past. I believe my isolation has accelerated my meekness. And it is not my doing, but through Christ alone.

CHAPTER 4: PURIFICATION

Removing contaminants

P urification is the process of removing contaminants or unwanted impurities from something. When we look at gold being refined, purification is such an essential part. After the isolation stage of removing the impurities, it's important to keep the purified state of gold separate from the undesired dross. Each step is vital to retain the overall refined process.

> *"It was beneficial for me to have been brought up in the church. That gave me a firm foundation."*

As a child growing up in the inner city of Boston, I did not know how to have a relationship with God. What does a relationship with God even mean? What did that really look like? I knew the 'Churchianity' thing to do, but what was a genuine relationship with God, and how would I obtain one? However, God is so good! Being raised in the church planted in me a firm foundation of knowing who God is. The isolation stage of life drew me closer to Him. I now know that He has been there for me all along.

There's an old poem my mother had in a frame when I was little; it's called *Footprints in the Sand*. The frame showed a picture of pairs of footprints on the beach along a coast. The footprints ended in just a pair, showing that two individuals started the journey, but in the end, there was just one traveler, who was God, carrying the second traveler up in His arms. The website, *poem4today*, credits a fourteen-year-old girl named Mary Stevenson, as the original author. In my refinement process, I imagine myself to be that traveler whom God picked up in His arms, from time to time, to keep me pure and safe from the threats of impurities I constantly attracted in my life.

There is a saying: God will not place more on you than you can bear. Although with good intent, I have often asked myself, how accurate is this? We say it, but is it backed up by scripture? God tells us to take up our cross and follow Him (Matthew 16:24), but this comes with being a Christian and denying ourselves. Life in Him is not about bearing our own problems and troubles. What He says, in times of trials and tribulations, is to cast our cares unto Him, for He cares for us (1 Peter 5:7).

When we cannot bear the hardships of life, the struggles, and worries of tomorrow, He says to not worry about tomorrow (Matthew 6:25). He tells us He will never leave us, nor forsake us (Hebrews 13:5). If He cares about providing the sparrows food and shelter, how much more does He care for us (Matthew 6:26)? He created us in His very image (Genesis 1:27)! When we cannot bear it on our own, that's when Christ comes and helps, if we ask Him. We think we are walking alone, but it is Him carrying us through the most difficult times. As long as we are seeking Him and His will, He will be with us. All we have to do is put our trust in Him and His Word. He is the way, the Truth and the Life (John 14:6).

The Bible says to humble ourselves under the mighty hand of God, and He will lift us up (1 Peter 5:6). The part we like the most is God lifting us up. However, it takes us humbling ourselves before Him. The book of James talks about purifying our hearts, all those who are double-minded (James 4:3). Do you know that a double-minded person is unstable in all their ways (James 1:8)? God is looking for total surrender unto Him. There's a book I once read, called *Lady in Waiting by Jackie Kendall and Debby Jones.* It's centered on Mary Magdalene, a woman in the Bible who poured the anointing oil at Jesus' feet—a symbolic preparation for His burial. However, the amazing part of this story is the cost of the anointing oil. You see, during these times, women didn't have much prestige or wealth to offer except for marriage and having children. They were submitted to their family until a desired spouse presented himself to her. With that spouse came financial support, as he would be the one to provide for the family.

In these times, what the women could offer was a *dowry*. A dowry was a payment from the family to the future spouse to help provide for the woman. Dowries were priced treasures. It was a very expensive perfume (or something similar) that the family would keep throughout the woman's lifetime until she was ready for marriage. This dowry was, in a sense, a woman's entire life savings and very valuable.

Imagine this: you meet someone and give them your entire life savings all at once. Something not only you, but your family has saved up for you to support your future marriage. It may seem reckless. But that reckless behavior is made perfect through the man, Jesus Christ.

The Bible says, if you lose your life for my sake, you will gain it (Mark 8:35, Matthew 16:25). God has given us a new life through Christ Jesus. We are not our own (1 Corinthians 6:19). When we give our life to Him, we don't doubt. We are not double-minded. We do not look back at the 'old life' and desire it, because we have become anew in Christ Jesus, our Lord and Savior. So, when you reflect or read about the woman coming to Jesus and pouring the oil on His feet and wiping it with her hair, think about that reckless abandonment of her old life. Is this something you are willing to do? This really stuck with me for some time. I wanted to be the woman who poured my all at the feet of Jesus. I wanted to give my everything to Him. If this is how you are thinking, then God has started to remove that stony heart and replace it with a heart of flesh. You are being purified!

> *"God showed me the right path to take,*
> *when I didn't know which way to go..."*

With purification comes a new mindset. As mentioned in the previous chapter on Isolation, one of my favorite verses of scripture is Ephesians 6:10-18. It is about placing on the armor of God. Through the years, I have learned that this is a daily thing that needs to be worn. Sometimes we do not know how or what to fight against without this armor. To be clear, this is not actually physical armor, but more so spiritual. Ephesians 6:12 states, *"We do not fight against flesh and blood but against evil rulers and authorities of the unseen world..."* One part of the armor we are putting on is the helmet of salvation. The thing the enemy loves to attack first and foremost is the mind. He doesn't know our thoughts, but he monitors our actions and motives. He and his imps have been studying families for generations. He knows where and how to attack.

However, he cannot do anything without authority being given to him. That authority is through us allowing and/or God allowing the enemy to attack us. I do believe that the helmet of salvation, if not worn correctly, is the first thing the enemy will attack in a Christian's life. Especially a new believer and/or one who is weak in their faith. His goal is to annihilate the threat, which is you and me. *"Why?"* you may ask. It's because we are being used as a vessel for the kingdom of God, to bring others to Christ.

A vessel is something that is being used and filled for a purpose—in this case, the Gospel. We are being filled, through the Holy Spirit, to be used in this way every day. The helmet is used to protect our mind, which is ultimately the heart, to include our will and emotions. If we have our spiritual helmet off, this gives free rein for the enemy to come in and plant seeds of doubt, fear, worry, and so much more. This is one of the easiest targets of the enemy. Once he has your mind, he has control of everything. With this comes a downward spiral of so many other things. However, once we recognize the spiritual battle, we can overcome whatever struggles or obstacles are in the way. We start to not look at human beings as the issue, but the spiritual operations happening behind the scenes, that we do not see with the naked eye. Placing on this armor of God needs to be done daily. The reason is that the enemy comes with different tactics and strategies to weaken our faith. He sends people and circumstances in our way to doubt the promises of God. This is the same trick he has been doing since the beginning of time. Why does he continue? Well, because it works. The attacks of the enemy are real! Unless guarded by the Word, many people fall into his deadly traps.

The Word of God is the only offense to these attacks. Going back to Ephesians 6, it is called the Sword of the Spirit (Ephesians 6:17). Oftentimes, we are on the defense and trying to protect ourselves. Just know we have the power, through Jesus Christ, to fight back against the enemy! This is why we need to be in the Word daily. This is not just for routine discipline (although important), but it is necessary for survival. Without it, we will repeatedly suffer defeat. There have been countless times when I forgot to place this armor on or pray and read the Word in general, there is a challenge or attack I face throughout the day. Although this can happen regardless, being spiritually unprepared is dangerous. Just think about it for a second. Would a military soldier go into battle without a weapon? In the majority, if not all cases, absolutely not! If so, then how would he be able to defend himself from an incoming attack? In the spiritual realm, this is just as important. But do not fear. The wisdom of God is far greater than anything the enemy can bring upon you! The Word of God says we are more than conquerors through Christ Jesus (Romans 8:37).

> *"Jesus came and set me free from the bondage of sin in my life."*

Purification is a beautiful part of the refining process. The Lord has allowed me to go through the steps of refinement to bring me to this point in Him. When I look back at the things He has done in and through me during this time, I can honestly say, *"Wow God, You are amazing!"*

I remember getting baptized in March 2012. It was a decision I had made on my own. No man or woman prompted me to do this. The Holy Spirit living in me did. I was making a public declaration to the world that I am choosing to follow Christ. I had been baptized in the church where I grew up in Boston. However, this time was different. As I walked up and sat in the water basin, the pastor of the church asked, *"Do you believe Jesus Christ is your Lord and Savior?"* I said a certain and heartfelt, *"Yes, I do."* Then, he looked me straight in the eyes and said, *"I know you do..."* That moment caught me by surprise. It was a large church, and I barely even spoke to the pastor. I realized it was not him saying this, but the Holy Spirit. God was affirming through him to show me I am His, and He knows me! It was such a precious, intimate moment I will never forget.

As I went down in the water and came up, I noticed my feet came up first. In that instant, I remembered my mother telling me I was a breech baby and that I wouldn't turn in the womb. The nurses were going to turn me, but at the last minute, I turned on my own. That moment of coming out of the water was a rebirth in Christ. The old was gone, and all things were being made new (2 Corinthians 5:17)! Little did I know about the journey of sanctification that would come with this. However, I was excited and determined to press on toward the mark of the prize in Jesus!

A necessary step in keeping pure was having accountability with like-minded people and being involved with activities that would draw me closer to Christ. Before having accountability, I was seeing this guy, who I knew was not for me. We will call him *GM*. Our 'situation-ship' was solely for physical pleasure. We started talking after one of my friends, who GM liked, decided she didn't like him. Not that I was that into him either, but more so I wanted to be the one he desired. Once my friend made it clear that she was not into

GM, that opened the door for a false acceptance from a man—something I had always hoped for. False, being that it had nothing of God in it. All of lust and pleasure.

As God was purifying me and giving me a new mind and heart, these sexual encounters that I knew were wrong would only bring about more guilt, rather than pleasure. At one point, I even ended up crying while in the act. God was calling me higher in Him, and I was in disobedience. The last time GM and I got together was my graduation night from pharmacy school. Even though I went through rededicating my life to God through baptism, I still needed healing and deliverance from many things. Sexual immorality was merely the surface evidence of certain issues in my heart.

Shortly after we met up that night, I realized I had to cut all ungodly ties. This was vital in order for me to have life in Christ. You see, sin brings forth death (James 1:15). There are times we do not recognize the consequences of sin. It is something that can spread like cancer. When we think of cancer, it is something that needs to be cut off or removed immediately. If not, it can spread and ultimately lead to serious health consequences, and eventually death. But how can you work on finding treatment or a cure if you do not even recognize it as an issue? Like cancer, we cannot deal with sin until we recognize it. That is step one.

During this time of refining, although God was removing so many things, I still had a taste and desire for sin. I wanted to hold on to it like it was my best friend. Why? Well, because I could honestly say I didn't trust God fully. At this time, I was still dealing with the desire to be loved. I didn't know how to tangibly feel this love without physical intimacy.

After graduating from pharmacy school, I stayed in Tampa, FL. That allowed time for me to reflect on certain things. When God is working on you, the situations and people you once enjoyed, you begin to no longer desire. With sin removal comes not only recognizing the issue but also the consequences, or what we would call the 'symptoms' in the pharmacy world. Like cancer, there are symptoms of sin that you realize need to be dealt with. There is something you need to be healed from. I ended up completely breaking off with GM. Not only via phone, but also through social media. It was difficult at first, but absolutely necessary!

God also started removing my desire to go to clubs. I remember going to a nightclub in Tampa, with a friend. I sat in the darkness, looking at the TV monitors hung on the walls. A song by a popular artist was playing, while her music video showed on the monitors. I saw the wickedness in the video and heard the demonic influence in the music. I noticed this had an influence on the environment within the club. In that moment,

I thought to myself, *"What am I even doing here?"* God had removed this desire of clubbing from me. I felt like a veil was lifted from my eyes. I was certain there was no reason for me to be there. That was the last time I can remember ever stepping inside a club.

In no time, I was moving forward to what God wanted me to do. When I finally made the conscious decision to follow Him—and I got sick and tired of being sick and tired, that is when God gave me the strength to move on. Before this time, I recall not having any respect for myself or my body. Now, I actually saw myself as pure. There was even a time when I went to church during an altar call. I went up front, heart pounding. I can't even remember what the pastor was saying. All I know was that I cried out, *"Jesus!"* and fell crashing to the floor in tears. God promises us in Isaiah 1:18 [NLT version], *"Though your sins are like scarlet, I will make them as white as snow. Though they are red like crimson, I will make them as white as wool..."* Praise the Lord!

Deliverance was taking place in this process. Chains were being broken! However, I still had self-confidence issues. This purification process would go on for years. There are some things that come off immediately, and some that take a little longer, and others even longer. There were many reasons why, but mostly trauma and even pride can hinder full deliverance. However, I knew one thing—that God was working all things out for my good (Romans 8:28)! He was seeing me through the process of deliverance that I needed. The freedom of the bondage of sin in my life. Sexual immorality was the surface of a deeper issue. God was showing me myself and things that needed to be purified. He was doing the purifying.

An important part of the purification process was addressing the feelings of rejection I felt in the relationship (or lack thereof) with my father. In middle school, my dad started reaching out, mostly via email. He kept this form of communication for some time. Eventually it grew into phone calls, and even visits. There was a time my brother and I spent Christmas with him and his 'new family.' I was excited to see my new brothers and sisters. However, it always felt as though I was imposing on a family that wasn't my own.

While visiting during Christmas, there was a time I was sitting at one end of the couch and watching my dad play with my little sister on the other end. I watched in envy of their relationship, wishing I had that type of intimacy with my father. As a grew older, the Lord opened the door of opportunities for me to share these feelings with my dad. Although I did not get the response I was expecting from him, it lightened the weight of rejection off me, and I soon was able to build the father-daughter relationship I have with him today. This process of building a wholesome relationship with my father would take years to nurture and is something I am still working on. As I matured in Christ, I realized that there will be people who fail me, and I will fail people, but God never fails (Numbers 23:19, Hebrews 13:5, 1 Corinthians 1:9). I have learned to be grateful for the dad I was given, and our relationship has grown so much! We recently ran a half-marathon together. Something I had always hoped and dreamed of doing with him. What an amazing God, to care about this detail of my life and see it come into fruition!

Relationships with women were a major challenge for me, before committing my life fully to Christ. Growing up, I didn't have the best relationship with my mother. She was my first example of a relationship with a woman. Although I love my mother dearly, she did many things to place distance between her and me. There was a time when we were visiting my family in Boston. My mother was at the doorbell, attempting to ring me in. Little did she know that she didn't release the intercom. With that, I heard her talking about me negatively to other family members. This really hurt. The person I thought to trust the most betrayed me in a way I never thought she would. It stuck with me for some time.

CHAPTER 4: PURIFICATION

The rocky relationship with my mother didn't start with her and me. She and her mother had arguments and disagreements. I recall a time when I was little, my mom stormed out of my grandparents' house. That was the first time I saw the frustration between the two of them. I didn't understand it then, but a generational curse had to be broken for me to move forward.

There were other things that caused our rocky relationship; however, I have given these situations to the Lord. At some point in my walk, I had to forgive her for the things that she had done to me. Why? First and foremost, because Christ forgave me. But also, I desired a relationship with her. She is my mother. As I was drawing closer to Christ and He was purifying me, I knew it was a command to honor my mother (Exodus 20:12, Ephesians 6:2). I wanted to do good by her. It was not for her benefit, but for mine.

As I honored and respected her, our relationship grew. As it grew, the Lord honored and favored me in life in so many ways. This small act of obedience allowed me to build relationships with other women, both young and older. However, God was still working on me.

During my purification process, even when I messed up and fell short, God continued to use me for His glory. I started getting involved in ministry. One ministry was with a group called Pinky Promise (PP). PP is a women's organization founded by Heather Lindsay that focuses on honoring God with your life and your body.

As I grew in leading women's Bible studies and ministry, initially, my heart posture towards them wasn't as loving. There was a time when one lady, who was a part of our PP group, was pregnant. Although out of wedlock, it was a blessing from the Lord. Another sister suggested we do a baby shower for her. At the time, there was a PP Statewide Baby Shower that was being hosted in Atlanta, GA.

I suggested we help the sister attend that baby shower. The only caveat was that we lived in Tampa, FL. One lady called me out and stated how frustrated she was by my suggestion of having the pregnant sister attend the statewide shower. Looking back, I was happy that she called me out. In my selfishness of not wanting to truly help the pregnant sister, I thought it would be easier to send her somewhere else so that I wouldn't have to deal with the situation. This was the truth.

I didn't know how to build relationships with women, let alone do anything for them. This helped me realize the lack of love and selfishness brewing within me. I had to recognize that these people were not the issue. Neither was it my mother. It was my own selfish ambition. God had to remove this major character flaw from my heart. He was pruning and showing me how to help other women. He taught me how to be patient, kind, and loving toward other women.

> *"Remove all the impurities from silver, and the sterling will be ready for the silversmith..."* (Proverbs 25:4)

In my professional career, I knew I had leadership talents and skills. I was in various leadership roles during pharmacy school and would become a professor at a college of pharmacy. I would even start-up and lead clinical pharmacy services in different places of employment. However, what did that look like in the church? I continued to connect with other PP sisters in the area. However, I could tell that God was leading me into deeper things in Him.

I started getting involved with the singles ministry at my church. At the time, I never heard of a singles ministry. But God had me there to learn more about Him and His character. One day, I was asked to speak at a singles ministry event. I thought to myself, *"I am not qualified; why me? There are so many other women (and men) who are more qualified than me to speak. Some have been a part of the ministry for a while. Some who have been following the Lord and/or attending church longer than I have..."* But, in obedience, I spoke at the singles event. This gave me the courage to give another talk. In that obedience,

God continued to bless and give me favor with leadership within the church. The Bible tells us that man looks at the outward appearance, but God looks at the heart (1 Samuel 16:7). God was calling me to speak.

Eventually, I was obedient to the call. I recognized it wasn't about me, but more so how God was using me, all for His glory. The Lord had given me the ability to use my skills from school, such as creating PowerPoint presentations, to prepare to speak, for such a time as this. Ironically, I spoke about something the Lord was doing in my life—sanctification. In preparing the presentation, I was growing in knowledge and understanding of the sanctification process in a Christian's walk.

There's a parable in the Bible about the men with different talents, and how the man with ten talents doubled his profit, and so forth. However, the man with three talents buried his talents. Because of this, God took his three talents and gave them to the man with the ten talents. The man with the ten talents knew how to be diligent with what God had given him. I see this for myself.

As I was obedient to the Lord in the little, He saw fit to continue giving me talents that I didn't even know I had. This opened the door for many other opportunities to be used by Him. After speaking at the singles ministry event, I found myself more willing to serve, which ultimately led to my being a part of the singles ministry board.

That propelled me into what God already knew I had: a gift of administration within the church. I learned so much about myself back then. With certain gifts God gives, it's important to stay humble and remember you cannot do it in your own strength. The Lord continued to show me, through ministry and using my spiritual gifts, that it was all about Him. I had to die to selfish ambition and pride, and submit to His perfect will for my life.

There were many other opportunities that the Lord led me to serve, more specifically with leading women and children, including The Lord's Prayer Ministries, WordToWomen, Club56 children's ministry, and more. The Lord gave me a heart for fostering and mentoring women— particularly younger women. He showed me how to pour into them. With the refining of character and pruning through sanctification, the Lord continued equipping and using me for His glory. Not only did I have a gift of administration and leading, but teaching other women and children came naturally to me. I enjoyed it!

There was a time, after graduating from pharmacy school, the church leaders asked all the graduates to go up to the front of the church for prayer. We received a gift from the youth pastor. After the prayer, one of the global mission's ministry leaders offered to connect for potential medical missionary work overseas. I thought to myself, *"Wow, things are looking promising. God is on the move!"*

However, my character still needed to be tested and purified more than I could ever know. If someone were to tell me the many trials and tests I would need to go through after that moment, I probably would have given up, turned around, and said, *"Never mind, I'll just stay right here in my unrefined/non-character-building state!"* However, God had other plans.

The gift from the youth pastor was a 'Christian' book (for the sake of the preservation of the Body of Christ, I will not share the name of the book) and a journal. I was excited to dive in and start reading the book, in hopes of further developing my spiritual maturity. I used the journal to jot down notes and prayer points while reading. At first glance, the book seemed very encouraging. I eventually shared about the book with my mom.

An attribute of my mother I truly admire is that she has the spiritual gift of discernment. If something doesn't sound right, she is not afraid to speak out about it. When I mentioned a part of the book that said to pray to God and ask Him to 'complicate my life,' she stated, *"That is something you should never ask God to do."* In looking further into the book, many parts included things like that of new age and witchcraft practices. I was shocked. How could something that was supposed to be Christian be so deceptive? Even worse—this was given to me by my youth pastor. Someone I thought I could trust to provide spiritual guidance.

I immediately took the book, tore the pages (so that no one else could read it), and threw it away in the dumpster. I confronted my youth pastor regarding the book on Sunday. Being in the early stages of my walk with Christ, it was not done with wise counsel or advice. I remember walking up to him before service to share what I felt about the book. His wife came up, and they both confronted me, yelling, with my back against the wall. I was hurt and in dismay.

I thought that if I exposed the book, then maybe they would apologize. Perhaps it was a mistake, and they didn't mean to give a book like this to the youth. If I showed them what the Bible said versus the book, maybe there would be an explanation. Yet all that I received was a finger pointing in my face, telling me how they knew the author of the book. I was shocked by their reaction. I had to then muster up the strength to walk into church service. I felt alone and upset. It was one of the most discouraging moments of my Christian walk that I could remember.

After this traumatic encounter, I stepped into the service thinking, *"I have to worship you now, Lord? How can I?"* That was my honest thought. It brought me down a lonely path in my life, questioning God and whether Jesus is the Way. Not that I stopped attending church, but I had to start doing the research for myself. I started questioning the Bible and if it was really authentic. I was looking for the truth.

I wanted to believe it, but how could Christianity be real when I received just as much hurt inside of the Christian faith as I did in the world (so I thought at the moment)? I remember sitting at a coffee shop, researching the Bible and its authenticity. I searched the internet for information about the Bible and its references to credibility. I learned about the Septuagint and the Dead Sea scrolls.

Through my research, I was hoping to find something that would prove this was not the way—just to validate my emotions. However, I couldn't find a single falsehood about the Bible. After all the searching, I came to realize this one thing is for sure: the Bible is more real than I could have ever imagined! This means that Christianity and being a Christ follower is the only truth.

This solidified who Jesus was to me. I stopped depending on people to validate Christianity, but went to the Author and Finisher of my faith, Christ Jesus, my Lord. This burned in me a desire to learn more about the Bible. From then on, I began an exciting journey that, until this day, I am still on. I am learning each day how to be a disciple of Christ and a reflection of who He is. What the enemy meant for bad, God turned into something AMAZING! He changed my entire perspective on what it meant to be a Christian. I had a desire and thirst for righteousness. I believed what the Word of God said about me. God revealed things to me I never knew about myself.

> *"It is important to stay*
> *pure in the sight of God."*

"Stand fast therefore in the Liberty wherewith Christ hath made us free, and be not entangled again with the yoke of bondage..."

(Galatians 5:1 KJV)

There was a time when a few other sisters in Christ and I went overnight camping. This was not something I normally would do; however, it was at the beginning of the pandemic, and it was a chance to get away from the city. At the time, I had recently moved to the DMV (DC, Maryland, Virginia) area. One sister was a very experienced hiker/camper and led the way. I was excited and somewhat anxious, ready to see what camping was all about. I went a few times as a child with the Jewish/white private school I attended in Boston, but never as an adult. As we prepared to leave, I had the slightest clue of what to buy or how to pack. My friends gave me some advice, but it seemed like an investment only if I would be doing this long-term. I took the easy route and purchased everything I needed through Amazon.

Driving to Shenandoah, Virginia, the views had me in awe of how beautiful God's creation was. The fall leaves' colors of the trees decorated along the mountain landscape appeared to be a painting and not reality. Nature seemed like a movie! So serene and calm. Like we were the only ones in the world out there. During this time, while sleeping in my tent, I had a dream that seemed more surreal than anything I had ever dreamed before.

Before sharing about the dream, I want to back up for a moment and talk about something significant that happened a few years back, prior to the camping trip. This will tie into my camping trip experience. There was a time I met a neighbor of mine. It was a casual encounter; however, as soon as I met him, we had an immediate physical connection. I made the initial mistake of providing him my phone number. I assumed he was married, and the purpose of providing my number was as an arrangement for his son to cut my front lawn. Although

I primarily provided my number for that purpose, we ended up casually texting. After learning of his divorce, I was still cautious about my encounters with him. The tempting physical attraction was obvious. James 1:14 says, *"But each person is tempted when they are dragged away by their own evil desire and enticed."* Then after some time, I gave in, and we went to the movies.

That day, the sensual, sexual intimacy was overwhelming. I knew I was in over my head. For reasons of my flesh, I still went out and spent time with him. I decided I would attempt to be the 'good girl' and invite him to church— something we would call 'missionary dating.' All the while, he was the one converting me towards a dangerous road to sin. He walked into church one Sunday during worship. The lights were dim, and I initially had my eyes closed.

When I opened my eyes, I was surprised to see him walking towards me. I turned to look at him, and his head looked as though it was the head of a serpent. I immediately jumped back in surprise and fear! I should have known in the spiritual realm what God was trying to show me about him. However, all the warnings in the world could not stop me as I continued to walk in the flesh.

After church, we went to the park, and on the way home, he attempted to kiss me. I pulled away; however, it was such a powerful, lustful moment that came over me that I kissed him again before getting out of the car. I couldn't believe what was happening. After all God had bought me out of, this is where I was? In a lustful encounter with my neighbor? My flesh wanted more; however, in my house, I had to pray and, thankfully, ended up receiving a text from a friend of mine asking how everything went.

The Bible says to, *"flee from sexual immorality. Every other sin a person commits outside the body, but the sexually immoral person sins against his own body. Or do you not know, that your body is a temple of the Holy Spirit within you, whom you have from God? You are not your own, for you were bought with a price. So, glorify God in your body..."* (1 Corinthians 6:18-20 ESV). I now understand why. It is like playing with fire. I didn't realize how fast the enemy would try to take hold of the situation. If you give him an inch, he will knock down the door. I knew I had to let this 'neighbor' go. However, I didn't know how to do this in my human strength, so I prayed for God to show me.

There was a time when I thought things were looking up, as we hadn't spoken in some time. Until one day, my grandfather (my father's dad) passed away. Although I didn't know my grandfather too well, it was still a vulnerable situation where I felt I needed the physical comfort and touch of a man. After coming home from the funeral, there was a sense of loneliness that I should have taken to the Lord. Instead, I called the 'neighbor.' I knew I would regret opening up this situation again. As I walked into his house, there were some things that the Lord showed me immediately that confirmed he was not a man of God (although I already knew this by his fruit).

We lay on the couch together to watch a movie. I remember thinking, *"Maybe this one time, it wouldn't hurt?"* Just as I began thinking this, my stomach ached. It wasn't a physical ache, but more so spiritual. I never knew what it meant to grieve the Holy Spirit, until that very moment. There was a still, small voice within that said, *"Honor your husband."* That voice shocked me. I wasn't thinking anything about a potential husband and had no prospects. However, my perspective immediately shifted. I ended up going home shortly after. A few months later, I moved from NOLA to Maryland, to never see him again.

Now, back to the dream on the camping trip. I had a dream about the guy. In the dream, I was in the tent, and there was a dark shadowy figure of him outside the tent. I couldn't see his face in the dream but knew by the dark figure who the dream was trying to portray. Although I was physically inside the tent during the dream, in the dream, I could see that this dark shadow of his was outside. The dark figure was attempting to pull a plug that was in my tent. The plug cord was one of those thick, orange, long construction-type cords plugged into a multiple-cord outlet inside my tent. I was trying to hold on to the cord and outlet as much as I could, as he was outside the tent, pulling. I woke up, knowing this was a dream symbolizing how the enemy was attempting to pull me from my relationship with God. This was an enemy of God, sent by Satan. I was holding on for dear life. Similar to how it was in reality when I met the guy. It was nothing but the grace of God that I did not fall completely into lustful sexual sin with him.

Through the purification process, the Lord showed me how much I needed Him in order to stay pure. It was not something I could do on my own. Purification comes through recognizing the deep, hidden sins of the heart. Only God knows our hearts, yet He is gentle and kind in taking time to reveal our own hearts to us. He then allows us to come to Him to change our stony heart into a heart of flesh, purified through and by the Holy Spirit. Purification is not a one-and-done. Oftentimes, there are layers to be stripped. As a Christian, the purification process of removing impurities will continue until our final perfected state is reached in heaven.

CHAPTER 5: REFINEMENT

Improving to make pure

R efinement is the process of improving something by making small changes to bring it to a fine or pure state. The refinement process for gold involves continuously placing it through the fire until it's at its best state. This process may require multiple attempts to remove all impurities. The refinement process takes time, with the end result being pure gold. Sometimes the temperature needed to refine gold is so hot that it can be uncomfortable or even dangerous for those handling the metal. However, once the fire dies down and dross skimmed off, the gold shines brighter than ever before.

God refines us over time, ensuring all impurities are removed, leaving only pure gold. He places us through the test and works in and through us to be refined.

"And I will put this third into the fire, and refine them as one refines silver, and tests them as gold is tested. They will call upon my name, and I will answer them. I will say, 'They are my people', and they will say, 'The Lord is my God.'..." (Zechariah 13:9 ESV)

The Holy Spirit plays a pivotal role in this process. He is our advocate and testifies of Jesus Christ (John 14:26, 1 John 5:6). Without the Holy Spirit dwelling in us, no true refinement would ever take place. The Holy Spirit is the *vehicle* of refinement. He carries us through the fire of tests and trials, purifying and refining our hearts so that we become more like Jesus Christ.

"I have gratitude in knowing that I am saved by my Lord and Savior."

There was a time I attended a women's conference where a pastor shared his testimony. In that testimony, he mentioned that he used to only see Jesus as Savior in his life. He knew Jesus died on the cross for his sins, but He wasn't Lord over his life. That makes all the difference! Many of us make this mistake in our Christian walk and oftentimes see Jesus as a savior or friend and nothing more. But do we really know who He is? He is more than this. As I developed my relationship with God, I got to understand not only who He is, but who I am in Him. Prior to this, my identity was in sports, being liked by others, relationships, school, and much more. I was searching for something or someone. It took time and patience for me to really dive into the Word of God and understand His character. Who is He in scripture? How does He speak? What is His reaction in certain situations? Who am I in Him?

I soon came to realize the character of God. He is not only Just, but Righteous. He is all-knowing (Omniscient) and all-powerful (Omnipotent). Through His Word, I learned He is loving and gracious, yet Holy and to be feared. As a child, I had such a thwarted view of God. My mom used to make us watch Left Behind Movies of the Rapture returning. I used to be afraid of this event actually happening, thinking I would have to suffer the grueling Tribulation to come. I used to think God was just a judgmental God, looking at all my wrongs and waiting to strike me down or return at any moment.

Then, came Christ in my life. He showed me He was there all the time, patiently waiting. He was in the jail cell waiting for me to sober up. He was in the five-car accident I had in undergrad, while the car was spinning out of control, protecting me from harm's way. He was at my lowest and highest points in life. I realized that I didn't have to try to build a relationship with Him. As I prayed and read His word, He would pursue me in a relationship with Him. He wanted to speak to me. He loved when I spoke to Him and shared my thoughts. Although He would already know what I was going to pray before uttering a word, He wanted to listen to me. After all, I am His daughter!

I learned how necessary it was to know my identity in Christ. There were verses I had to speak over my life to heal from the identity society expected of me, called me, or who I thought I was. I started speaking my identity in Him over myself. A few scriptures on identity I have memorized over time included my being a co-heir with Christ (Romans 8:17), adopted into the family of God (Ephesians 1:5), and part of a royal priesthood (1 Peter 2:9). Through refinement came the manifestation of change, and the new creation that God had called me to be.

> *"Kneeling shows your heart posture toward God; complete surrender to Him."*

An essential point I want to talk about before this book is complete is the intimate relationship with God. During the different refinement processes, God was always there. As I was being sanctified and refined, my relationship with Him was developing and maturing. I have noticed that there are different stages in my relationship with God. This does not mean that my walk with Him is stagnant, but that there are distinct periods and seasons of my life in which I need Him in specific ways.

For example, there are times in my life where I can't seem to get a word out. These are times I would just sit and listen to Him, read His Word, pray (internally), and journal. There are other times when there is so much excitement and outward praise toward Him. Sometimes I just worship, praying aloud to Him, thanking Him aloud for all He has done. Sometimes in my walk, I need Him and me to just be together. No talking, no music. Just Him and I. Other times, I just want to cry out to Him and pray in the Spirit. Sometimes I feel alone. However, there are intimate moments in my walk where things shift. Any or none of these can be circumstance-driven, but mostly how the Holy Spirit is leading me. I'm cautious with going by my feelings and emotions. If I did, I would not have continued this journey for long.

A key element in developing intimacy with the Lord is to learn obedience. To go past what I feel. This is usually a time when the Holy Spirit is guiding and helping me. These are the more intimate moments of my life. His strength is truly perfected in my weakness (2 Corinthians 12:8)!

"Likewise, the Spirit helps us in our weakness. For we do not know what to pray for as we ought, but the Spirit himself intercedes for us with groanings too deep for words." (Romans 8:26 ESV)

The Holy Spirit showed me what the scripture reference above looked like in my life. There was a time when I was in church, during my last year of pharmacy school, and going through so much in life. It was a season of my life when I was dealing with severe cystic acne. It took a toll on my self-confidence, and I felt that every time people looked at me, they weren't looking at me, but they were more concerned about the acne.

During church service, someone sang a song. I felt a spiritual release specifically during one part of the song, as the lyrics written by Katie and Bryan Torwalt filled the air, *"We give You praise and all of the honor. You are our God, the one we live for. We give You praise and all of the glory God..."* Somewhere deep in my spirit, through the struggles and pain of life, I belched out a loud cry. It was a cry I never would forget and only seldom have done again. It was like the Holy Spirit was interceding at that very moment for me. I remembered the scripture on how the Spirit prays for us in our weaknesses. At such a weak point in my life, I needed the Holy Spirit to intercede, and He did! I didn't recognize at the time the deep refinement that was taking place in me, through the Holy Spirit.

> *"I now can share the Gospel and reach so many younger women."*

With refinement comes responsibility and discipline. My refinement period coincided with my transition to residing in Maryland. God was taking me into even more uncomfortable situations. My desire for intimacy with Him was becoming stronger. I desired to go deeper into the Word. However, how was I to go about this? I soon was led to do more evangelism (sharing the Gospel). This was during a time when I wanted to learn more about the Bible.

Going to church and my alone time with God was good; however, there were questions I had about the Bible I wanted to understand further. Sunday sermons and Wednesday Bible studies weren't enough. I had the yearning to learn more. I began researching an online course through Christ's Forgiveness Ministries, founded by Pastor David Lynn, in Toronto, Canada. There was a free online class called Phase One Discipleship. It was the answer to what I had been praying for! During the course, Christians from all walks of life, all over the world, would get on Zoom every Saturday morning for about eight weeks and learn how to evangelize and operate in their spiritual gifts. I was eager to sign up!

Pastor David was an amazing teacher. We would listen and soak up all the wisdom he shared about the Word and his personal life experiences. It was like living out the Bible as a real disciple! I felt blessed and honored to learn from such a mighty man of God. This was one of the most monumental times in my life, truly diving into the Bible and understanding its truth and how to apply it to my life.

I would learn about strongholds and deliverance in a Christian's life, and how to walk a life of freedom in Jesus. There were assignments where I had to go out and share the Gospel of Jesus Christ. One time, I went out alone near my neighborhood. I ended up meeting a lady who was Catholic. I shared with her the truth of the Bible and that there was only one mediator to God the Father, the man Jesus Christ. After being fully equipped with the understanding of His Word, there was a fire from the Holy Spirit that began to burn in me to go out and share more of the Gospel of Jesus Christ.

Before the discipleship course, God was leading me to evangelize. I remember the first time going out to hand out gospel tracts. It was with my mother. We headed out to our local shopping center.

I was nervous, since we didn't know what to expect. I also never had the training or skills of what to do. Although no exciting moment took place, it was a small step in the direction God wanted me to go. This would be the beginning of many opportunities to share God's Word with others. After the discipleship course, I continued to evangelize. I saw myself being bolder and more fearless. I was on a spiritual high, and nothing could stop me! Soon after moving to the DMV area, I got connected with a local church. I wanted to ensure the church had a heart for lost souls and for sharing the Gospel as I do.

I believe God called me to the DMV area to be a light in the darkness. The DMV differed from other places I have lived before. In NOLA, the spiritual wickedness of the area was out in the open. Almost like people were proud of their Voodoo and witchcraft. However, in the DMV, more specifically DC, I recognized the spiritual darkness deeply rooted in the city.

There would be times I would drive into DC from Maryland, and I could feel the spiritual shift in the atmosphere. This shift is something I can't really describe in words. I felt it was a gift of discernment that God had given me. The only way to really stop these forces of darkness was in prayer and fasting. There would be moments when I questioned why I moved. Then, I realized God was using these situations to refine me. He saw fit to bring me to live near the nation's capital to do this! I look back at moments where I preached on the steps of the Lincoln Memorial or spoke to someone about Jesus in front of the White House. I am honored and humbled by the mighty hand of God in my life. These were exciting moments of God's refinement and how the Lord used me mightily to share His Word and my testimony, all for His Glory!

In sharing the Gospel, I have been able to minister and be an example to so many other women. God has led me to witness outside of nightclubs. When I go, I am intentional about my physical appearance, being modest in how I dress. I do this to set myself apart and let the women who are going to nightclubs see a distinction with how a godly woman should dress. This is not to shame them, but to visually be a light in the darkness.

When I used to be in the clubs, I remembered how I would dress. Super short dresses, low-cut shirts, and high heels. This was what I thought was cute and attractive. If I had a woman come to evangelize to me in a long, flowing dress, completely covered, that would stick out to me. *"Why is she different?"*

Speaking of the club, there were times when God had previously called me out of the darkness of the club. There was a time when I was standing outside in line. A short distance away, I saw a guy dressed in a suit, standing in front of what seemed like a church. He opened the door, and the light inside was very bright. I was immediately drawn to the light. It was dark outside, after all. I felt a gentle nudge to go towards the guy. However, I wasn't ready. I still had the desire and taste for sin.

I see my evangelizing in front of the club to be something similar. Often, I would get stares, but interestingly, mostly respect. People were intrigued that someone would be so bold to stand outside a club and share about Jesus. However, little did they know that was exactly where I needed to be. I would share about Jesus and how women should dress and present themselves. I shared my testimony of how I used to be in the club and how God changed me. Many listened, while others mocked. But seeds were being planted. The Bible says that one water, the other plants, but God gives the increase (1 Corinthians 3:6).

You may recall a story in the book of Daniel regarding Shadrack, Meshach, and Abednego. This was during the times when the king of Babylon required everyone to bow to him when he was present. At this time, the three men of God refused to bow to the golden statue that King Nebuchadnezzar had built. After the king found this out, he was furious and ordered them to be thrown into a fiery furnace. Similar to Daniel, these men were not afraid of the ramifications that would come with not abiding by the authority of the king. This act of bold faith turned into them coming out without even the scent of the fiery furnace on them. These were men who stood the test of time and had Christ at their side.

Similar to the story of Daniel, it is a time we are living in today where we should not bow to a golden statue, king, or any other thing or person besides God. Sometimes I had an encounter that was not as detrimental or dangerous but where I had to stand firm in my faith.

I can recall when I was an indoor cycling instructor at a local gym. I played Christian music, but upbeat, to keep the cadence going. One day, someone reported to my supervisor that I was playing Christian music. My supervisor asked if I could avoid playing any such songs. I respectfully declined the request. I explained to her that if people can play worldly music, like Rhianna and Jay-Z, I can play Christian music. I continued to play Christian music during my spin class until leaving the gym for a separate reason. This may have seemed like something small, but God honors the small victories for standing firm in Him.

I remember another situation, working as a pharmacy technician at Publix while I was in undergrad. My supervisor requested that I work on Sundays. I knew Sundays were my day to go to church, as it was vital in my spiritual walk with Christ. It was necessary to have off on Sundays. I took a stand and used religious reasoning as to why I could not work on this day. In my past and current positions as a pharmacist, I occasionally led patients in prayer or shared the Gospel with them. These were all risky situations that could have cost me my job and maybe even my career. I even had a chance one time to pray for a woman who claimed to be a witch doctor. The enemy has no power over Jesus! Through it all, my refinement was coming to fruition.

So, I ask you, how are you standing the test of fire? What is holding you back from going all in for Jesus? The word of God says, if you lose your life for my sake, you will find it (Matthew 16:25). I can tell you firsthand that finding Jesus has been the best thing ever. What's the point of being in the race if you're not going to fight? Stay faithful to what He has for you. I want to clarify that the only way you can truly go through the test of fire, similar to Shadrack, Meshach, and Abednego, is by having Jesus standing with you! You cannot fight this battle alone.

> *"I am saved by grace,*
> *through faith in Jesus Christ."*

Salvation is a free gift. When you think of a gift, you think of something exciting; maybe you don't know exactly what the gift is yet or how to use it. Do you know that being saved through Jesus Christ is the best gift you will ever have? Better than any gift you can imagine. Think about the best gift you have received or would like to receive.

In comparison, salvation is infinitely more valuable. It is the gift of eternal life through Jesus Christ. He is the Lamb that was slain before the foundation of the Earth. Growing up, my mother would always mention that *"Christ died for me."* She would say, *"He hung on the cross over 2000 years ago, and although He was in the worst pain and agony imaginable, He thought of me!"*

It took time for me to really understand what she was saying. Christ knew me before I was even formed in my mother's womb (Jeremiah 1:5). He knew that I would come on this earth and that I would need a savior. Even more important, that He loved me enough to die on the cross for my sins. We all need a savior. The Bible says that we have all sinned and fallen short of the Glory of God. We were born into sin. Because of this sin, there is separation from God.

There is no way to have true peace except through God. Jesus Christ is the Prince of Peace. He will never leave nor forsake us (Deuteronomy 31:8, Hebrews 13:45). So, how do you earn this free gift? All it takes is faith.

Without faith, it's impossible to please God (Hebrews 11:6). The Bible says that if you confess with your mouth that Jesus is God and believe in your heart that He was raised from the dead, then you will be saved (Romans 10:9). It takes repentance—which means to completely turn from your old way of life of sin, to Christ. The amount of faith depends on how much you trust Him. Do you trust Him in your finances? Do you trust Him in your relationships? Once you build that trust is when faith steps in.

Faith shows us that we, in our own efforts, cannot change things. It takes committing our ways to Him in order for our plans to succeed (Proverbs 16:3). When you make that commitment to God through faith in Him, you are justified (made right) through Christ. With that justification comes sanctification. Sanctification begins the process of refinement.

As a Publix pharmacy technician, we had this free antibiotic program. If a patient had a prescription for antibiotics and it was on the list, we would process the prescription under the program. There was a wide range of customer reactions to the free program. Patients would come up to the counter and ask, *"Why is this free?"* Other patients would request their provider to write a prescription just because it was free. People have different reactions to something being free. Some are cautious, awaiting that "catch" to the scheme, while others go all in, trying to get all they can out of it. That's similar to how some may approach salvation. Since it is a free gift; many may ask a similar question as to *"why"* or *"how?"* Being skeptical of the whole thing.

However, when Jesus reveals Himself to you, you know that this gift of salvation has nothing to do with a sales gimmick. You can't use human logic or effort to attain this free gift. It is only through the Holy Spirit. All you need to do is accept the free gift He is offering through faith in Jesus Christ.

> *"I will trust in the Lord and lean not on my own understanding."*

As mentioned, trusting in the Lord increases your faith in Him. Everything else makes sense when you trust Him to work it all out. It's better to trust in the almighty God than in our own understanding of what we think we know He can or cannot do. I have had times where I thought, in my human way of thinking, that I knew what was best for me. Sometimes, I thought that God was, in a way, punishing me, because I didn't understand what He was doing in a situation.

There was a time when I was finishing pharmacy school, and everyone was getting postgraduate residency training interviews, except me. Residency training was something I really wanted. It was the 'ideal' route to go as a pharmacist if you wanted to work in the hospital setting, doing clinical work. It seemed like all the pharmacy students I knew were getting interviews with different residency programs.

It felt like I was missing out. I couldn't understand why the Lord would not bless me with getting even one single interview. One day, I was so upset about the situation that I shouted out, alone in my living room, *"Why didn't You choose me, Lord? I'm Your child?!"* I thought God was punishing me for something I unknowingly did. Little did I know, a year later, I would get the residency I desired, in His timing!

The Lord opens doors for us on His terms. Looking back, I realized I was not ready for a residency training. God had to still prune some things out of me in my character. I am grateful that He does not go by my timing. He has His own way of doing things, all for His glory and my good.

Do you feel like you are in a refinery season? What things are you struggling to trust the Lord in? Maybe a house or a husband? Children maybe? A new job? I am here to tell you that when you trust in God's perfect plan for your life and submit to His will, all things work together. It takes time and patience to perfect this trust. The Holy Spirit has helped to comfort me. Oftentimes, I would forget what God has and can do, and lean on my own understanding. Even currently, I am still awaiting God's timing in my life for things I have prayed for years about. However, I am learning that God is more concerned with my spiritual state than my physical. He cares about pruning my character to prepare for heaven, rather than giving me the cares of this world. Like the loving Father He is, He does not always give me what I want but does always give me exactly what I need.

There is no formula for getting what you want from God. It is more so allowing Him to shift your focus and trust in His will for your life. I have learned that His plans and will are far more perfect than I could ever imagine. Sometimes, I get discouraged and forget. However, I turn to His Word, and it always recenters my mind on Christ and His promises to me.

> *"If someone wants to argue or quarrel,*
> *let them have it and give it to God."*

One of my favorite books in the Old Testament is the book of Proverbs—mostly because of its emphasis on wisdom, knowledge, and understanding; things that God is continuously refining in me. The book of Proverbs applies to how we act and react in almost every situation and circumstance. I believe God intentionally created thirty-one chapters of Proverbs so that we have no excuse from utilizing His wisdom accordingly.

Wisdom, knowledge, and understanding have different meanings, yet they relate to each other. Knowledge is something you attain. One can attain knowledge through studying or reading. For example, in school, you attain knowledge of a subject by reading the class material. Understanding is the next level. Once you have attained the knowledge, understanding comes through grasping the concept.

Now that you have read the material, do you know what that material means? What is it saying? Can you explain the material in your own words? If you can, then you understand the information. Wisdom comes from applying knowledge and understanding. Once you can relay the information in your own words, are you now able to do what you have attained through understanding and knowledge? Are you able to live that information out? Having previously worked in academia as a professor, I can tell you that the wisdom of how and when to apply knowledge and understanding is a difficult thing to do.

In looking at this as it pertains to the Word of God, it's even that more difficult. Many people have knowledge of the Bible and may even understand it to the point of explaining it to others. However, when it comes to the wisdom of applying it throughout their daily lives, that's where people fall short. James 1:23 reads, *"For if you listen to the word and don't obey it, it is like glancing at your face in a mirror. You see yourself, walk away, and forget what you look like..."*

The most important part of the refinement process is obeying God's Word. This is true wisdom. The Bible says that obedience is better than sacrifice (1 Samuel 15:22). It was the obedience of repentance from King David that made him a man after God's own heart (1 Samuel 13:14). It was the obedience of Esther to listen to her cousin Mordecai's promptings of approaching the King on behalf of her people, the Jews. So much more comes with obedience. In John 14:15, the Lord says, *"If you love me, you will keep my commandments."* The Lord's commandments are not burdensome (1 John 5:2). His commandment is to love Him with all your heart, mind, soul, and strength and to love your neighbor as yourself (Mark 12:30).

I encourage you to read a Proverb a day, for God to enhance your wisdom, knowledge, and understanding in Him. With wisdom comes refining in character. One issue I have often struggled with is my words—what I say and how I speak to others. I am originally from Boston, so it's safe to say many of us 'Northerners' have this issue. Oftentimes, I would say things without thinking and experience the consequences later. In the book of James, it tells us how dangerous the tongue is, corrupting the whole body (James 3:6). God had to show me that not only my heart needed changing, but my mouth.

Although I would be honest and truthful in *what* I shared, I did not have a filter in *how* I shared things with others. The Lord continues to work on this in me. I have learned to use wisdom with my words. Praying and reading God's Word helps me with sharing things, as led by the Holy Spirit. At times, I mess up. But God is gracious and is showing me how to improve in this area of my life.

Just as a doctor writes a prescription, God's Word serves our spiritual, mental, emotional, and even physical health. If I were to translate this into a 'prescription,' so to speak, it would be written as such:

R_x

Patient: _____

_____

Prescription:

Drug Name: The Holy Bible

Directions: Meditate on one scripture twice daily, morning and evening, as directed by the Great Physician

Use: For the relief of depression, anxiety, or any other signs/symptoms of sin

Side effects: None

Benefit: Refining of character and instructions to eternal life

Additional instructions: Please use in combination with prayer and fasting, as directed by the Holy Spirit

Refill 1 2 3 4 5 Infinite

This prescription could motivate you to read God's Word. Trust that He will see you through life's most difficult challenges, refining you along the way. Remember that refinement is a continuous process. It will never be fully complete until heaven. Are you ready to make the commitment? If so, use this 'prescription' to keep you accountable. If needed, even consider printing your name on the line where it says 'Patient.' Trust that He is and will continue to extract, isolate, purify and refine you. All for His Glory, and your good!

CLOSING REMARKS AND PRAYER

A s you finish reading this book, take some time to journal and reflect on the goodness of God and what He has brought you through. Who has He been in your life? A Comforter, Keeper, Defender, or Friend? Maybe He has been more than one of these. Or maybe He has been all the above. I suggest going through the different sections of refinement and jotting down some things about your process. Search the scriptures to see how God has taken you through each process:

Journal Reflection Points

<u>Extraction</u> (taking or pulling out something, especially using effort or force): *Consider and reflect on how God has refined you. What has He done in your life to make this possible? How and what did it take to bring you to where you are today, in Him? What parts of you still require extraction?*

_____

_____

_____

_____

_____

_____

_____

_____

_____

_____

_____

_____

<u>Isolation</u> (separation of one substance from another to obtain a pure or uncontaminated state): *What does the isolation process look like in your life? What people, places, or things have God isolated you from and why? During that time, what were things that God was trying to show you about yourself and about Him? What was the outcome of this isolation process?*

_____

_____

_____

_____

_____

_____

_____

_____

_____

_____

_____

_____

_____

_____

<u>Purification</u> (the removal of contaminants or unwanted impurities from something): *What are some things that need to be purified through the fire of the Holy Spirt (e.g., impure thoughts, feelings, emotions)? How can you relate this back to your extraction and isolation process? Share any scripture reference points that may come to you during this time.*

_____

_____

_____

_____

_____

_____

_____

_____

_____

_____

_____

_____

_____

_____

<u>Refinement</u> (improving something by making small changes to bring it to a fine or pure state): *How has God used the refinement process to direct your steps and draw you closer to Him? What fruit has come of this refinement (e.g., ministry, church leadership, community involvement)? What other refinement is needed?*

_____

_____

_____

_____

_____

_____

_____

_____

_____

_____

_____

_____

_____

_____

Now that you have journaled and reflected, take a few moments or more to pray, praise, and worship. Lift Jesus' name up high. He is worthy of your praise! The Bible says, if we don't praise Him, the rocks will cry out and praise Him (Luke 19:40). Do not let the stones cry out! He is worthy of your praise. Exalt Him! He has done so much in and through our lives. May this book be a testimony to you of His goodness and mercy. How He can use a girl from the inner city of Boston to minister to you right now. A girl who never really knew her identity until she knew the Creator of identity—the Creator of all things!

My prayer for you is that there will be a chain reaction of testimonies birthed after reading this book. Don't hold back! Share all that Jesus has done in your life. Give Him the Glory. One thing I should mention when sharing your testimony is that sometimes you may be afraid of who will hear and what they will think. That is understandable, as we continue to fight and wage war against our flesh.

Take some time to reflect. Certain things need to come through healing prior to sharing. The journey is not a sprint. You are running a marathon. Take time and allow the Holy Spirit to speak to and through you. This had to happen for me in order for this book to be birthed forth. Years of refinement were needed before I could finally muster the faith to write.

There will be ups and downs, but keep pressing in. The journey of sharing your testimony may not look like mine, but it is perfectly designed to reach the people it needs to, how and when it needs to.

Maybe you're an artist, public speaker, or teacher. Either way, the goal is to share about the refining process He has bought you through! Glory to God, hallelujah!

Dear Lord Jesus,

I thank you so much for the person reading this book right now. This was not an accident but a divine appointment by the Holy Spirit for me to be used to speak into their life. I am so humbled to be used as a vessel for Your glory, Lord. May You get all the Honor. I decrease, and may You increase. I pray that You purify them through the fire of Your Holy Spirit. I speak LIFE into them right now. Depression has to flee! Doubt has to go. Pride we rebuke in Jesus' name. I pray against the attacks of the enemy in their life. His assignment on their life is up. No weapon formed against them will prosper! I pray right now that You put a blessing and hedge of protection over them and their family. Increase their faith and trust in You. They will be overcomers by the Blood of the Lamb and the word of their testimony.

In Jesus' precious, holy, and mighty name, I pray. Amen!
Blessings,
Sis Rita

www.ingramcontent.com/pod-product-compliance
Lightning Source LLC
La Vergne TN
LVHW041222080426
835508LV00011B/1042